It Was All a Game Until…

By Jacqueline Russell

It Was All a Game Until...

Copyright © 2012 by Jacqueline Russell

It Was All a Game Until...

Printed in the United States of America

ISBN 978-0-9852094-3-8

All rights are reserved solely by the author. The author declares that the contents are original and do not infringe on the rights of any other person.

No part of this book may be reproduced in any form except with permission from the author. The views in this book are not necessarily the views of the publisher.

Scriptures taken from the King James Version ®. Copyright © 1982 by Thomas Nelson, Inc. Used by permission. All rights reserved.

Scriptures taken from the THE HOLY BIBLE, NEW INTERNATIONAL VERSION®, NIV® Copyright © 1973, 1978, 1984, 2011 by Biblica, Inc.™ Used by permission. All rights reserved worldwide.

Scripture taken from *The Message*. Copyright © 1993, 1994, 1995, 1996, 2000, 2001, 2002. Used by permission of NavPress Publishing Group."

Reference to Single, Whole and Holy (Christian Women and Sexuality) by Joy Jacobs and Deborah Strubel.

It Was All a Game Until...

Autograph Page

Autograph this book as a personal investment to yourself or the life of someone that God has put in your path on this life journey.

It Was All a Game Until...

Acknowledgments

"For I know the plans I have for you," declares the LORD, "plans to prosper you and not to harm you, plans to give you hope and a future." **Jeremiah 29:11**

I am eternally thankful to my creator for all that he has done in my life. For it is a constant reminder that without him I am nothing.

To the man that God prepared for me and me for him, my husband. Thanks for inspiring me to write and keep writing. You are the epitome of what each woman strive to have as a mate in their life. Your love, meekness, and pure heart makes my heart smile each and every day. I love you not because I need you, but I need you because I love you!

A very special thanks to my daughter that has always inspired me to want to do and be the very best me I possibly could. The love that I have for you has strengthened me in ways that I could never believe were possible.

To my mom, thank you for teaching me to be a diligent worker. You always taught me to work for what I wanted and to be steadfast in doing so. I am so thankful that even in those times that you had to work and couldn't take us to church; you always had someone that would step in and fulfill that role in your absence.

It Was All a Game Until...

To my Dad, thanks for loving me unconditionally, and being supportive of me and my dreams.

To all of my siblings, especially Tammy, thank you for all the fights and disagreements we had growing up as it made us have a bond that is inseparable. I love each and every one of you with the purest love. I continue to pray God's blessing upon you.

Thanks to my church family, FMBC for being supportive in all my endeavors. I love you all so much.

A heartfelt thank you to all my friends that supported me and my daughter in more ways than one. To Coretta, Debora, Deniese, Jo, Joannie, Lena, Lil', Mary, Pearl, Phyllis, Ruth, Sherry, Stacey, Toyia, Vicki, and Vonda I love you all so much. You have all inspired me in many ways to just do me, in my way. I thank you for loving us.

I sincerely thank the Late Ms. Peggy Womack (Ma' Peggy) and Mrs. Joyce for embracing me and my daughter and treating us as family. You loved us because it was always so easy for you to love anyone that crossed your path. We love you!

To Elder Virginia thanks for allowing me to be a part of "AW'SOME" Ministries. Being in the company of such awesome women of God has really been an amazing experience. God has really anointed you and I pray that He continues to bless you as this organization continues to move forward in the work of Lord!

To Stacey, thank you for wanting me to be a part of "Esther Outreach Ministries, Inc." This ministry has become such a vital part in my life. It has allowed me to grow in more ways than one. I love you and continue to allow God to use you!

Finally, thank you to True Perspective Publishing House, Sean Cort for believing in me and allowing me to make this a reality.

I would also like to express my gratitude to all of those that supported me in all my endeavors throughout this journey thus far. I am forever grateful to you!

Note to my Sister

This book is dedicated to every woman that uses games as a way of dealing with her life issues. Life is not about who can beat who, but it is about how well you accept responsibility for what you do and move forward. Many times you feel that you have to be better than the next woman to get a man to notice you, but in reality the only man that you need to notice you, is Jesus. When you truly decide that enough is enough, I mean truly decide that, then and only then will enough be Enough!

It Was All a Game Until...

TABLE OF CONTENTS

"The Outlook of the Game" 3

"The Onset of the Competition" 7

"The Change of Venue" 13

"Home Again" 19

"I Do, but I Really Don't" 23

"Life with a Hustler" 29

"The Tables Turn" 37

"Baby on Deck" 51

"Games, Games, and more Games" 57

"Losing becomes a reality" 63

"Changing the Game" 75

"The Reconstruction" 85

"God Delivers" 99

Introduction

Growing up on Compton Circle in the country town of Elba, Alabama, where the roosters were the alarm clock and the mid-week game of Old Maids was always the excitement of the day, proved to be some lessons that Joslyn Burns wouldn't soon forget. She was one of six sisters and three brothers that she had to compete with concerning everything.

By the time she made it through grade school, high school, and subsequently to adulthood, Joslyn had labeled herself the winner in every situation at all cost. Competing with her siblings was one thing, but when she used that same game mentality in every aspect of her life, she found that the games got tougher to win and the lessons behind the games were even harder to comprehend. Everything was definitely a game to Joslyn until…

It Was All a Game Until...

It Was All a Game Until...

CHAPTER ONE

"The Outlook of the Game"

*C*ompton Circle was always full of kids laughing, screaming, and crying and this gave off the sound of the female worker bee sucking nectar to make honey. On the contrary, on this unforgettable Saturday evening when the bright, orange sun was just setting below the trees and the cool breeze of spring was crisp in the air, the sound that filled the air would put even Joslyn in a melancholy mood. The music that old man Gentry was playing on his juke box talked about how a man loves a woman. Joslyn skipped over and asked Mr. Gentry to turn it up so she could hear the words to this song because the passion in the man's voice made the song seem so sad.

The man singing was letting the world know that when a man loves a woman, he can't keep his mind on anything else and he'll trade the world for the good thing he's found; and if she's bad he can't see it, because she can do nothing wrong and he will turn his back on his best friend, if he puts her down. This song must have had some great meaning to it because Joslyn walked away thinking, one day, I want a man to love me just like that.

Being only in grade school and nine years old, Joslyn was very observant of adult situations while playing with the kids in the neighborhood. She would play house with girls, pretending to cook light, green oak leaves as collard greens in one of her mom's old foot tubs and used the stiff, orange clay from the street as cornbread baked in a rusted pan that had been thrown out by someone else's mom. Unlike the girls, when she played anything with the boys it had to be a game where someone had to lose. Joslyn knew that no matter what she had to do, she had to be the winner because after all, no man would want to love a woman that didn't win.

While observing the adults, she saw how the men would be with the other woman across town on Green Street while their wives or live in sweetheart would be at home with the kids. At some point he would get caught and the women would fight for what seemed like eternity, while he stood on the sideline observing and smoking something rolled up in a piece of brown paper from that week's grocery bag. It was alarming to see these women continue to fight day in and day out; and for what, over a man that didn't seem to want to do what was right. These experiences put a stake right through the message that she had heard in the song.

It was not supposed to be like this and the man certainly wasn't supposed to have more than just one woman. Immediately, at that very moment of filtering through her thoughts, the not so obvious became obvious and the seed had been planted. Joslyn came to the realization that life was full of games and that she had to play them in such a way that made her the center of attraction and ultimately the winner.

It Was All a Game Until…

CHAPTER TWO

"The Onset of the Competition"

*B*eing one of the most underdeveloped girls physically in Elba High School, made Joslyn work extra hard in other areas that would make her stand out. She was an all-around athlete that excelled in volleyball, basketball, softball, and track and field. She would be one of the most recognized athletes in south Coffee County.

Upon approaching the eleventh grade, Joslyn began to realize that she had a small fan club that consisted of boys throughout the small county. Not really the savvy girl when it came to matters of boys, she would pretend to ignore the gawking because she didn't know how to handle the situation while being in their company. It made her feel uncomfortable trying to hold a decent conversation with the opposite sex. However, as the year progressed, she was able to embrace the attention like she was an Oscar winning actress strutting down the red carpet in hopes of receiving that little gold plated figurine for her accomplishments.

Somehow this became the focal point in which she made competition a life strategy. It didn't matter to Joslyn what the challenge or circumstance would be, or the fact that being in a competition that someone would lose; what mattered was that she had to win or simply appear to have won and that was that!

Joslyn knew that using competition as her life's strategy would take some careful manipulation and some strategic planning to always be ahead in the game. After all, she had seen how men played the field, misused, mistreated and hurt their counterparts and she refused to be another notch in some ones belt at any given time. Therefore, sports became the tool for which she used to see the manifestation of the competition in rare form.

The girls' basketball team always had to work the concession stand and the entrance gate during the Friday night football games. After Joslyn and her comrades shifts were over, they would sit in an area where they could see all that was happening on both sides of the field. The Elba Tigers were playing a team from the West side of the county, the New Brockton Gamecocks, when in walks this gorgeous boy with a girl that was tall, shapely and not so cute on his arm.

Ashley yelled out "Hey Tristan"! He returned the greeting and continued to walk with the girl holding his arm. The competitive nature in Joslyn quickly rose like black eyed peas boiling over in a steam pot. Her thought was, find out his complete name and let's get this ball, in the hoop, at the buzzer.

When Ashley said his name was Tristan Carter, and that he played the saxophone at his church where his dad was the pastor, that was enough said. Joslyn told Ashley and the others that he would indeed be her boyfriend. They all laughed because they felt that it was virtually impossible because she didn't know him. Ashley was from the west side of the county. Not really caring what they thought or said, Joslyn let them continue with their verbiage of doubt while she was plotting her quest for the ultimate dance in the end zone.

As time went on that year, Joslyn continued on her path at winning the game of life. She was definitely developing as a young woman and her medium frame had become proportioned to that of an hour glass. She hadn't made contact with Tristan as yet, but the game was still on. The remainder of that school year ended and the beginning of the new school year was school as usual.

Everyone always had new clothing that they exhibited at the beginning of the school year. The girls came to school sashaying in their new Jordache and Sassoon jeans and the boys strutted in their Wrangler jeans. Joslyn decided that she would wear her old clothes from the year before, while everyone else was wearing their new ones. This would once again set the stage of her being the center of attraction when she wore her new clothing later. It became apparent to Joslyn that the game was much bigger than she imagined originally. Not only did she have to win the game of life, but, she had to become more skillful than anyone else playing it. Joslyn had transformed into a person that would stop at nothing to seek out and conquer any challenge.

The football season had come around again and the focus was once again on getting Tristan as she had stated before. Joslyn and her comrades went to the weekly hangout at Mickey D's as everyone did after the games. Upon approaching the side door of the restaurant, Joslyn noticed Tristan standing with a group of homeboys by the fountain drinks. She knew that she needed to act fast because he was not with any female. He was with his friends and this made it fair game in her eyes. She flounced over and introduced herself to him. He was intrigued with her wit and smile, as she was with his, and the game began.

The time spent dating Tristan, was more of a game than she had anticipated. Even though he said that he was no longer dating anyone , there was really no way of Joslyn knowing if that was true because of his distance from her and his closeness to the other chic. But time would reveal what the real story was. Tristan was indeed still seeing her and made no excuses for it and Joslyn didn't ask for any. She was going to win him at any cost and her competitor being somewhat of a factor in the equation, was irrelevant.

However, relevance did come when she found out that Ms. Not So Cute wasn't the only competitor that she had to contend with. Tristan was proving himself to be a real Casanova. There were several at her school that she knew were after Tristan and some that even proclaimed to have had liaisons with him, but that didn't matter to her because in her mind it was just that sort of thing that would ignite that competitive fire even more.

Joslyn had such a competitive spirit about herself that she stayed in the game, refusing to lose to any of them. After all, neither of them could possibly be of her caliber. Joslyn was so caught up in the game itself that she disregarded what road this could eventually lead her too.

It Was All a Game Until...

CHAPTER THREE

"The Change of Venue"

*G*raduating high school was exciting for Joslyn, so the next phase of her life would definitely be interesting. She was heading off to Tuskegee University on a softball scholarship. Joslyn was thrilled to be going, but knowing that she was leaving Tristan behind at the local college, worried her after the latest turn of events. Joslyn and Tristan vowed to write and call each other, said their goodbyes, and she was off to the big city of Tuskegee.

Upon arriving on campus, Joslyn was aghast by the presence of the abundance of ravishing guys that she saw. They were of many diverse cultures and lifestyles. She thought to herself, "Tristan who"! Although she cared a lot for him, she knew that this college experience would be one to remember.

The first semester was difficult as she really didn't want to be there and missed Tristan terribly. So, she spent her time doing what most college kids do; she went to class, parties and hung out with friends on a daily basis. At the end of the semester, while on winter break, Joslyn decided to go home with friends and not tell Tristan that she would be home. It was basketball season and many tournaments were going on around the county. Joslyn decided to go to the tournament that was being held in Tristan's city. When she arrived at the game she noticed Tristan's truck in the parking lot.

She was so excited that she rushed past the people hanging in the lobby by the concession stand so she could go in and surprise him. When she entered the gym, she saw Tristan hugged in a tight embrace with the same tall, shapely, and not so cute girl, and she appeared a little larger than she remembered for her small frame, especially in the tummy area. Joslyn was stunned and at a loss for words. She was feeling a sense of loss.

It wasn't a sense of losing him to her; it was a sense of not winning all together. Joslyn didn't want anyone to see the hurt in her eyes so she left the tournament and went to visit a close friend that lived nearby. By the time she reached her friend's home, Tristan was pulling in the driveway as well. He was trying to offer her an explanation, but Joslyn acted as if it didn't matter. He admitted that she was pregnant and that it was his. Joslyn was hurt and angry with him, but she accepted what was happening and continued to date Tristan.

After the winter break, Joslyn returned to school with a new attitude. The events that had taken place when she went home, made her see that she had to be more vigilant when competing in some situations. She had to make sure that she wasn't going to put herself in any more situations where she would feel any hurt. Even though, the hurt feelings that she was experiencing were already a major thing happening in this relationship with Tristan, she was in some strange sense of denial that she could control everything from this point forward. This eccentric way of thinking was all due to who she had become.

The warmness of the sun on that clammy, spring afternoon made softball practice somewhat unbearable. The season had started and she really didn't like having to practice during the sweltering time of the day, but she knew that Coach London didn't care what any of the players thought or felt for that matter. The greatest thing about the season starting was that it gave Joslyn something to focus her attention on instead of speculating and being concerned about the issues with Tristan.

It became apparent that focusing on softball wasn't enough, so Joslyn decided that she would get out there and date. She would see Tristan when she went home to visit and date while she was in Tuskegee. This plan worked great, until Joslyn met this strong, handsome and smooth football player named Vincent. Vincent was about 6 feet tall with charcoal, black wavy hair that was manicured with the sharpness of a new razor. His body was as smooth as melted chocolate being prepared for dipping strawberries and his muscles, especially that ripped six pack, sent every waking sense in her body into overdrive. Vincent made

It Was All a Game Until...

Tristan seem so extraneous. He was nice and they could talk about anything.

Neither Joslyn nor Vincent asked the expected question, "Are you seeing someone"? Most guys don't care if you are, but most girls would want to know that; however, Joslyn really didn't care if he was or not because after all it was about her. Later on, he callously confessed to Joslyn that he was dating someone and that she lived in the same dorm as her. This tad bit of information really was trash to Joslyn because it didn't matter.

Joslyn didn't have a personal phone in her dorm, so she frequently used those mounted in the hallways. So, when Vincent wanted to call her, he had to call the phone in the lobby of Weatherly Hall and ask for her. The person answering would then transfer the call to Joslyn's floor. When Vincent called Joslyn a few weeks after they had begun spending a lot of quality time together, something unexpected happened. The girl that answered the phone recognized his voice because she and his girl were very close and they would double date all the time.

The girl waited until he asked for who he was looking for and then she asked if it was Vincent. At that moment, he recognized her as well and hung up. The friend quickly told Vincent's girl that he was trying to see someone in their dorm; and Vincent quickly warned Joslyn that she would stop at nothing to find out who it was. Vincent's girl and her friend went on what some would call a witch hunt trying to find out who she was.

Later that evening, as Joslyn entered the laundry room in the basement of Weatherly hall, she was approached by two young ladies that she had not recognized. One was medium brown, tall and slinky and the other was a chocolate brown, medium height and very round. When they spoke to her, the tone of the slinky one was that of a country house wife and the other was rough and ghetto.

They asked if she knew someone named Vincent and if she knew someone named Roslyn that lived in that dorm. Joslyn knew right away that they had the name all wrong, but as a part of her game mentally, she offered them help in trying to find out what room Roslyn stayed in and told them that if she found out anything she would get back to them.

Neither Reba McIntyre nor Sister Soulja had even thought to ask Joslyn her name. This interchange gave Joslyn such a natural high, that she actually stood in her mirror cheesing and clapping as to give herself a standing ovation. Joslyn didn't realize that she was becoming more and more of a game player while she was the one being played in each situation.

Joslyn told Vincent what happened and he said that he needed to do what was right by her because he had just learned that she was pregnant as well. This was double jeopardy to Joslyn as she had gone through this with Tristan. However, in this case, she respectfully discontinued seeing Vincent as she knew it was really the right thing to do.

The remaining months of her freshman year at Tuskegee wasn't all that great and Joslyn didn't want to return to school after summer break, but how was she going to tell her parents that.

CHAPTER FOUR

"Home Again"

*J*oslyn had just returned home from Tuskegee University for summer break, when she was told that Tristan was now a father. Although, she had spent time with Vincent and it was a mess, this made her want to prove something to everybody. She decided that if Tristan came to visit that she would tell him that they could work things out even though he had this child with the other girl. Later that week, he did come over and they agreed to work things out. Joslyn knew that this would be a new type of competition because it involved a child and she hadn't thought it through thoroughly.

As time sped by, Joslyn knew that she had to tell her parents that she didn't want to return to school. She had to come up with a reason that held some validity in order to get her parents to agree. Although she knew the real reason was to be there with Tristan, especially since that baby was in the picture. She had to make sure that he would be with her and not his "baby mama". However, she did understand that he would have to see her because of the baby, but that was as far as it would go.

Joslyn told her parents that school was too difficult for her and that she was going to flunk out anyway if she didn't come home. So, with that said, her parents told her that she had to get a job, because she would not be able to sit around and do nothing. Getting a job wasn't a big deal to her because she had worked her first job when she was 14 so this would be a breeze. Joslyn found a job with some friends of hers cleaning rooms at Elba's East Gate Inn.

The pay wasn't that great, but it was a job. During this time, she became aware that Tristan was not being totally honest about what he was doing. He had stopped going to the local junior college and had taken courses at a vocational school to become a Security Officer. He was now employed with an agency and making a substantial amount of money during that time. Joslyn was confused at why he kept this a secret as they were supposed to still be together. His explanation was that he wanted it to be a surprise. His reason really didn't make sense to Joslyn but as usual she accepted it.

After working for a few months, Joslyn and her mother went and got her a vehicle. It was nothing fancy, just a little blue Toyota Corolla. This was a stepping stone for her because now she could go and see Tristan and not have to wait for him to come visit her all the time.

It Was All a Game Until...

In August, on a Saturday afternoon, Joslyn had spoken to Tristan on the phone and they chatted about lots of things as usual. They would always talk about their dreams of doing this or that and just life itself. Joslyn never told Tristan that she had gotten her car that she named "Lady Blue". So, she asked what he was doing that afternoon and he said that he would be staying home because he just wanted to relax and that he would see her on Sunday afternoon. So, Joslyn said okay and they said their goodbyes and hung up.

She hurried and got dressed because she wanted to surprise him with her new car. She wore a leopard print, form fitting sundress with the back out and black sandals that showed off her nicely French manicured toes. Joslyn would never go anywhere without looking Diva luscious because she had an image to uphold, if only to herself.

It would take 45 minutes or more to get to Tristan's house depending on the traffic. When Joslyn arrived on his street, she could see from a distance that there was a guy and girl leaning up against a car in front of his house. Joslyn wanted to speed up but had to keep herself composed because real ladies don't lose their cool. The closer she got, she realized that it was Tristan hugging and kissing his baby mama.

At first, Joslyn wanted to drive by and go park and cry, but then the game in her came plunging forward and she had to stop the car. Tristan and his baby mama were looking at the car in suspense because they could not see who it was through the tinted windows and they hadn't seen that car before. Joslyn steps out of the car; Tristan's expression was that of a frightened child watching a horror movie. She asked Tristan if she could speak with him and his baby mama instantly answered no. Joslyn didn't really want to have a confrontation with the baby mama, but she was taking it there.

Tristan just stood there and Joslyn said okay, so answer this, "Who do you want?" Tristan looked at her and then Joslyn and said, "sorry, my baby's mama." At that moment, she began to repeatedly call Joslyn obscene names and leaped towards her as if to inflict some bodily harm. Joslyn's reaction to what she did was unexpected.

She immediately pulled out a weapon and told Ms. Baby Mama what would happen if she even thought about it. Then, and only then did Tristan decide to intervene in this ruckus. He didn't say much, he just grabbed her hand as they sauntered into the house together leaving Joslyn standing dazed and dejected near her car.

Joslyn felt that there was something déjà vu about what happened. It seemed like she had witnessed this many times before. After taking a careful inventory of the event, she realized that she had become one of those same women that she had witnessed as a child in many of the community love triangles before, verbatim. The competition and game playing had gotten a little harder to contend with and Joslyn didn't know how to process what was happening.

CHAPTER FIVE

"I Do, but I Really Don't"

*a*fter the altercation with Tristan's baby mama, Joslyn figured that even though she loved Tristan, he clearly couldn't feel the same way or maybe he could. She was always lying to herself about situations because it gave a sense of being in control of them. Tristan appeared at Joslyn's job trying to make her understand why he did what he did. He stated that he said all of that and acted that way because he didn't want her to put him on child support. He said he figured that as long as he spent time with her and pretended to be with her that she wouldn't do it. Joslyn understood the whole child support situation, but pretending to be with her was something that she just was not comfortable with.

Her thoughts were running wild at that moment. How could she allow that and give the impression that she had lost? She would never lose in such a way at any cost. Joslyn gave Tristan the okay and acted as if all was fine, but knowing deep within that there was something really wrong with this mode of thinking on her part.

Tristan began spending more and more time with his baby mama and Joslyn decided that she would find someone to occupy her time. So, she started going and hanging out more with her friends. When Tristan got wind of what was happening, he wanted to shut it all down. Tristan was over there playing Father Knows Best with his baby mama, but didn't want Joslyn seeing anyone but him. At that moment, Joslyn knew that she had won yet again. She had won his emotions and knew he would ultimately start to spend more time with her.

Tristan started coming around more frequently, but ironically Joslyn really didn't feel him as much as she did in the beginning, but she certainly didn't want him with his baby mama or anyone else, so she continued seeing him.

Joslyn discovered that she was pregnant weeks later and didn't know what to do. She was so terrified about this situation. She told Tristan that she was pregnant and he refused to hear it. This truly caught her off guard because they had been together so much lately and she really thought that they were going to be together, even though she didn't feel as much in love with him as she had before. Tristan was adamant about not hearing about the pregnancy and totally refused to see or talk to her.

She could not understand this change of events. She knew that he didn't want any more kids any time soon because he was already a teenage father, but she thought that in light of them becoming so close and spending time together that he would accept the idea gracefully. She couldn't have been farther from the truth. Tristan had become really mean about it all and totally flipped out. He stopped coming around and told his family that Joslyn was not and could not be carrying his child.

Joslyn was really upset by what Tristan had told his family and knew that she had to do something about it. She was only 19 years old and at that point in her life she knew that having a child would bring on many challenges that she wasn't ready to handle. She rationalized the pros and cons of her circumstance and decided that she would terminate the pregnancy. Joslyn was so hurt and scared all at the same time because she never thought she would be in this situation.

She spoke with her parents in regard to her situation and her parents advised against what she had planned to do. They told her that she would be okay and that they would make it work, but knew that it was ultimately her choice because she was of legal age to do so. Joslyn's way of thinking about this whole situation was so distorted by her desire to not lose.

She knew that if things remained as they were that Tristan would trot back over to his baby mama and leave her hanging with all the responsibility. She really could not let that happen. Not only could she not handle the responsibility at that time to care for a child, more importantly, in her eyes, she couldn't allow his baby mama to feel that she had taken him or won by any stretch of her imagination. Therefore, Joslyn decided to go ahead and terminate her pregnancy.

Joslyn went through the phone book trying to find a doctor's office that would assist in the termination of her pregnancy. She eventually found a doctor in Atlanta, Georgia, which was more than 7 hours away to do the procedure. She scheduled her appointment for the following Monday. She and her sister Faith drove to Atlanta on the Saturday before the appointment to relax and to give her time to think about what she was going through with.

On Monday morning, Joslyn went to her appointment. She felt devastated that she was going through with it. She felt even worse as she had to walk through the protestors and having them yell obscenities at her. Once she made it in the office, the procedure was completed fairly quickly and she would be on her way home in a few hours. Joslyn had to wait a few hours to make sure all of her vitals were great and that everything else was okay.

Four hours later, Joslyn and Faith were on their way back to Alabama. So many things were running through Joslyn's mind as she lay back on the passenger's side as her sister drove home. She resented Tristan for not being the man he should have been. She was upset that he accepted his baby mama when she had become pregnant and supported her decision. She couldn't help but think "Why was he not as supportive with her"? "What made him flip out and become so mean about the situation"? Joslyn needed answers to these questions and would stop at nothing to get them.

After being home for a week and recuperating, Joslyn decided that she would call Tristan. She wasn't sure if he would answer, but she knew that she would keep calling until he did. Tristan answered on the first ring. Joslyn was uncertain what to say when he did because quite frankly she didn't expect him too.

Tristan spoke first and asked how she was doing and that he missed her. Joslyn was confused about the missing her statement as he very rudely told her that he didn't want to talk to or see her for that matter. She told him that she was okay and that the ordeal has really done on number on her psychologically.

Tristan didn't care to hear about Joslyn's feelings or what she went through, he was just glad that she hadn't given him another child to pay for. All Tristan wanted to know was when he could see her again. Joslyn was very angry with Tristan, but when he stated that he wanted to be with her, she thought once again that she was in it to win it. They began seeing each other again and Tristan alluded that he was in love with her and wanted to spend his life with her. But, Joslyn wasn't really sure about all that because even though she loved him, she wasn't totally in love with him anymore.

A few months down the road, Tristan showed up at Joslyn's job and asked if she could leave work early and she said yes. Tristan took her home to shower and get dress and told her that he had a surprise for her. After getting dressed, they drove down town Enterprise, Alabama to the Circuit Court. He said hurry and come before we are late. Once inside, they rode the elevator to the fourth floor and entered into the door that read Marriage License.

She was mortified because she had not planned on getting married to anyone this way. Tristan began filling out the required documents and Joslyn just sat in silence because she had so many things going through her head. She did love him, but not to that capacity at that point. She didn't want anyone else to have him because that would mean that she'd lost at something. This was truly overwhelming to her as she stared blankly into space.

She was brought back to reality, when she felt a poke from the pen when Tristan thrusted it into her hand to sign the documents. She hesitated just a moment ignoring the voice within her, and signed the documents. The Justice of the Peace performed the ceremony for them. At the precise moment Joslyn said "I do", she knew that she really meant she doesn't.

CHAPTER SIX

"Life with a Hustler"

Joslyn was now Mrs. Joslyn Carter and with that came more of a game than she really was willing to play. By this time, Tristan had quit his job as a Security Officer and had decided that he wanted to make fast money. He had started gambling for fun with friends in the neighborhood, but after some time, he proclaimed himself as a professional gambler. Tristan had obtained this strange attitude about working, stating that he did not want to work for anyone. This would have been easy for Joslyn to accept had he finished college or had the means to go into business for himself, but neither of those applied.

Tristan began staying out all times of the night and not really making any excuses about doing so. Joslyn was working here and there. She may have a job at this place one minute and then decide that she didn't want to work there and get another job. Nonetheless, she would always be in a position to earn her own money.

After a while, rumors started to surface about Tristan and many different women. Joslyn would never really confront him with what was being said; she would just do her own investigations to see what she could find out. One Friday night, Tristan and Joslyn decided to go to the local hangout across town. This is where all the hustlers would hang out and the groupies would be on the prowl too.

When they arrived, Joslyn saw her good friend Marion standing by her car and walked over and started talking with her while Tristan stood by the car and had a few beers with his homeboys. Marion and Joslyn greeted each other with their usual hug, as this was customary for good girlfriends, and began talking about everything from cooking, to no good men.

Marion began to tell Joslyn of the rumors that she had heard about Tristan and the baby he was supposed to have on the way with Sheila, the girl that lived next door. Joslyn couldn't believe what she was hearing because the thought of Tristan having yet another child on her was more than even she could take, game or not. Not to mention, how he treated her when she was pregnant. After a lengthy conversation with Marion and getting all the facts that she needed, Joslyn told Tristan that she was ready to go home.

Upon arriving at their apartment, she asked him about the rumor. Normally she would not ask questions; she would get more information first, but this involved a potential child and she couldn't wait for this to explode in her face. Tristan denied the rumor and told her that she could believe it if she wanted too. Joslyn knew within herself the truth and said no more and went to bed. As time passed, it was something that just didn't seem to be right in Joslyn's spirit. Even though Tristan denied the baby thing, she was convinced that he had to have been involved because what woman would say that she is having a man's baby if she had never been with him intimately.

    The next morning, Joslyn replayed the conversation over again in her head and decided to go next door and simply ask Sheila about the rumor. To her surprise, Sheila admitted that she was indeed pregnant and the baby was Tristan's. Joslyn was in total disbelief because how could she not know that he was sleeping with the woman next door.

    Joslyn asked Sheila many questions about when and where she and Tristan had this affair and to her amazement; it had been in their home as well as Sheila's. At this point, Joslyn only said thanks to her and left. She went to Tristan and confronted him with this accusation. Tristan still denied it all and said, yet again, you can believe whatever you want. Joslyn was so confused and hurt because this was not the type of game or competition that had winner on it; this had Loser all over it.

    For the next several weeks, Joslyn was trying to figure out what to do about this issue with Tristan and Sheila. She didn't want to leave to go to work most days because of the fear of him having her in their home. Her thoughts were totally consumed with all that Sheila had told her. She contemplated on leaving him, but decided against it because she refused to lose to someone like Sheila.

She wasn't the reddest apple on the tree and she certainly wasn't of her caliber. Joslyn would never have Sheila utter the words to anyone that she took Tristan from her. Therefore, she would work through this situation as it came.

Several months had passed, and Sheila had given birth and moved across town with another man. Joslyn was happy about that because it meant that she was moving on and away from her husband. However, shortly after Sheila moved, Tristan was notified with a summons to appear in court for child support.

Tristan continued to say that this was not his child and that he wasn't with her. Joslyn just couldn't understand why Sheila would lie. It had to be true, because this would be devastating for Sheila if it turned out that he wasn't the baby's father after all.

Tristan requested a blood test after she insisted on it. When rumors surfaced that the results were back, Joslyn didn't wait for them to come in the mail. She went to Sheila and asked her what the results were because she needed to know. Sheila stated that the test revealed that her child was not Tristan's and that she was sorry for what has happened. Joslyn was relieved that it was not his baby and at that point in her mind it really didn't matter if he was with her or not because that was over now. Joslyn didn't realize that this was only the beginning of a long list of affairs that Tristan would have on her, but she was soon to find out.

Tristan really didn't care what Joslyn thought or felt because he continued to do what he wanted to do and she had no say in the matter. Month after month, Tristan would get accused of being with different women and would deny it and Joslyn would go through the whole process of investigating, only to find out that what Tristan was being accused of was true.

Joslyn started to realize that this life with a hustling man was not all that and the material things that came along with it started to mean very little. Tristan would often take or send Joslyn on shopping sprees whenever a rumor would hit the fan about him and spend an astronomical amount of money on whatever she wanted. Joslyn never noticed that this was a form of pacifying her, until one day while she was shopping at Nordstrom she saw one of the women that Tristan had been rumored to have been with.

As Joslyn shopped, she noticed what the woman was purchasing as well as what she was wearing. The woman had a short, A-symmetric hair cut with side burns, a gold pair of hoops on, and a spinning ring on her right index finger all which resembled Joslyn's hair style, earrings and ring. It was one thing to have an extramarital affair, but to groom the woman to resemble her was a little much. Joslyn continued to observed this woman as she shopped being careful not to alarm her that she sees her. However, when the woman spotted her, she began to speak very loudly in the store to the clerk to be sure that Joslyn heard her conversation. She discussed how she was seeing this married man and how he takes good care of her.

Joslyn was appalled to hear what she was saying, because after all, who would tell a stranger such things. The woman continued to speak about her life with this man and the clerk continued to be amused by the information. After listening for more than ten minutes to this mockery, Joslyn decided to purchase the items that she selected.

Upon approaching the counter, the loud mouthed woman approached as well. Joslyn acted as if she didn't notice the woman standing next to her when the clerk asked if she would be paying with cash or charge. Joslyn said, "Cash" and proceeded to pay for her items. As the clerk bagged Joslyn's purchase, the lady says to Joslyn "your hair is nice, and your earrings and ring are simply gorgeous, did you purchase them at Fox Jewelry in the mall?"

Joslyn knew that she was trying indirectly to inform her that Tristan had purchased hers too because that was his Jeweler. Joslyn said, "Yes" as she turned and faced the woman, piercing her with a stare that could kill. Joslyn stood and stared at the woman for at least thirty seconds before turning and walking away.

It Was All a Game Until...

After arriving home that evening, Joslyn knew that she needed to question Tristan again about this woman and the fact that she had things that resembled hers. Joslyn walked into the bedroom and Tristan was getting dressed to go out. Joslyn told him of the events at Nordstrom and Tristan denied even knowing the woman.

Joslyn knew Tristan was lying for sure because he attempted to use the same ole' pacifying strategy as before. In the middle of the disagreement, Tristan offered to purchase the new couch that she had been asking for that he'd already told her that she had to wait until later to get it. Joslyn told Tristan that she didn't want the couch anymore and that she had grown tired of the lies and games.

Tristan disregarded everything that Joslyn was saying and walked out. Tristan had gotten to the place that he did what he wanted, when he wanted, talked to Joslyn in such a disrespectful way and was very abusive verbally, mentally and sometimes physically if she said too much. Tristan had been allowed to do so much to her because she was so focused on winning that she was totally removed from the reality of what was really happening.

The many times that Tristan had been with other women and had been accused of everything from sleeping with them in their apartments, paying bills for them, going on mini vacations and fathering their children you would think that she would have walked away long before but she wasn't going to give anyone the satisfaction of uttering "she'd lost". However, she had come to the realization that the game was not working in her favor at this particular time and she knew that something had to change soon. Joslyn had heard many times the women in her neighborhood say that" if you can't beat them, join them". Joslyn had rationalized to herself that she had to do just that. She had to settle the score, win or lose, the game was headed in a different direction.

CHAPTER SEVEN

"The Tables Turn"

Joslyn started working out again and getting herself in tip top shape for settling this score. She noticed that she had packed on a few pounds over years because of the stress and emotional eating from all the drama with Tristan. Joslyn had always kept herself together with how she fashioned herself and her hair was always on point. She just needed to get those athletic legs and thighs back along with her firm backside.

After several weeks of working out at the fitness center, Joslyn was turning heads left and right. Men would approach her each and every time she went to work out. However, Joslyn wasn't going to settle the score with just anyone, she would choose her candidate carefully.

One afternoon, as Joslyn was picking up a prescription at Fred's Pharmacy in Elba, she ran into a very attractive man that she had heard so many of her friends take note of. Her friends thought that he was the most attractive and admired man in Elba. He was tall with jet black, wavy hair. His body was scrumptious and those nicely tone arms and bow legs were something that would send any woman's hormones into overdrive, especially when he was wearing those Wrangler Jeans. So, when Joslyn saw him waiting in line to get a prescription as well, she decided that she had to do something or say something to get his attention so she could have a conversation with him.

As she was thinking of a way to strike up a conversation, he turned and asked her about the pharmacy and how long does it normally take them to fill a prescription. At first, she was a little thrown off by his question because she was in a daze contemplating on what she would do to get his attention. He then cleared his throat and asked again and this time she had realized that he wanted to make conversation with her as well.

She told him that they were pretty good and reliable and under her breath she murmured "so was she". He turned around and continuing waiting in line but she noticed that he had a smile that was so big that she could see his cheeks extended from the back of his head. Joslyn knew then that he had heard her comment and that was the bait that she needed. After she got to window and picked up her prescription, she turned to leave and he was standing outside the door waiting. He approached her and they had a general conversation about superficial things.

Joslyn knew that his strategy was to get in a conversation with her with the hopes of them having more and she was definitely on the same page. After conversing for several minutes, she knew that she would be seeing him again for certain because the interest on both parts had become inevitable. He received a phone call and they departed without exchanging numbers, but Joslyn knew that was only a minor setback and that she would have that taken care of in no time at all.

Joslyn continued to work out, shop and read to keep her mind off of Tristan and all that he was taking her through. Even though she had a game mentality in the sense of staying with this man because she didn't want anyone else with him, she was totally miserable. Joslyn had gotten to the point where she began to dislike Tristan a great deal. Although, she loved him, she didn't like what he was doing and how he just totally disrespected her time and time again.

Joslyn would rarely hang out with her friends during this period in life because she didn't want to hear any negative things that she knew she would. Tristan was always with someone and Joslyn knew it. Tristan would come home time and time again with candid apple red passion marks on his neck and many times his clothing would be on backwards and/or the wrong side. He would tell Joslyn that he pinched himself or that he had his clothing on that way when he left home. Joslyn was at a point that arguing about the lies wouldn't change the facts, so it became pointless to do it anymore.

Tristan had become so much of a womanizer that he had started dating women from their very community, not to mention several so called friends. Tristan never cared how it made Joslyn feel because he was satisfying his own desires and never once noticed how what he was doing was causing a major shift in the dimension of their marriage.

Joslyn was so tired of feeling alone and lonely with a man that clearly couldn't love her the way that she needed to be loved. Although, she had everything that she wanted materialistically, she had no peace or satisfaction in this marriage. Joslyn had decided that she would seek out to give this mystery man her number to call her.

Joslyn was going for an afternoon walk when she ran into Hampton, the mystery man's friend. She asked if he would pass her number along to him and he said, "Yes"; and then asked Joslyn if she really wanted to do this as he knew her husband and she said "yes indeed".

After several days had past, Joslyn had not received a called from her mystery man, so she decided that maybe that was God's way of letting her know that it was wrong. Although, Joslyn wasn't living her life as a Christian should, she did believe in the Trinity; God, the Father, Jesus, The Son and The Holy Spirit. She was raised in the church and believed all that the bible said concerning God, Jesus the Holy Spirit and Eternal Life.

Joslyn knew that what she was contemplating was not that of God, but she wanted instant gratification because it seemed that nothing that she had prayed for was working out the way it should. Joslyn needed to feel like someone care for and needed her. She needed to know that she could win this game of life as she had set out to do. At the very moment she was thinking this, the mystery man calls. "Bingo", Joslyn said in her raspy, but captivating voice as she answered the phone.

Bingo, what does that mean, he said in a tone of curiosity. Joslyn told him that Bingo means that you are the winner of some kind of prize doesn't it and they laughed and talked for hours about his life and her very unhappy life.

Joslyn soon fell head over heels for this mystery man that she called Baby as his pet name. Joslyn began to do things that Tristan wasn't prepared to experience yet along accept. Joslyn became an equal to Tristan and his shenanigans. Joslyn had become so wrapped up in this love affair with this man, when she found out that he was married and had children. Joslyn was a little dismayed as she learned this information.

She remembers telling Baby about her marital situation and how unhappy she was from the initial conversation, but she never even thought about asking him about his status. Joslyn was so caught up in this relationship that it didn't matter that she was married or the fact that he was because she once again felt that she was winning. The ironic thing about it all was that she felt like she was getting back at Tristan, but he had no idea what was happening.

Even though Joslyn said it didn't matter about Baby's wife and children, she couldn't help evaluating the situation because she knew how she felt when it happened to her, but Joslyn couldn't bring herself to end this mess that she was getting deeper and deeper involved in. Joslyn would rationalize everything to suit the purpose that she set out to accomplish no matter how outlandish it appeared to be.

Tristan got wind of what was happening from his gambling friends and didn't hesitate to ask Joslyn about her indiscretions. Joslyn was so boastful to Tristan when she admitted that she was having an affair. She told Tristan everything that she knew would hurt him and make him feel what she had been feeling over the nine years that they had been together.

Tristan was so hurt that he even stated that he would hurt her and the man that she was seeing if he ever saw them together. Joslyn really didn't care what Tristan thought at that moment because she was so full of herself and the fact that he was getting it in his back side good! The table had finally turned on him.

Several months had gone by since Tristan had found out about Joslyn's indiscretions. He was so upset that he traveled to this underground gambling house in Ozark, Alabama to scout out new games and of course new women. Whenever, Tristan would go out of town to a gambling house he would be gone for months. Joslyn didn't care what he was involved in at this point because she was so consumed with her own extramarital affair. She and Baby went on about their interest in each other until Baby realized that Tristan was gone and Joslyn had all this free time. Joslyn wanted to spend every waking moment with Baby, but soon realized that this was virtually impossible because he also had a family to contend with.

Even though he had confessed his love to Joslyn, he would not and could not leave his family. Joslyn became very angry at the fact that Baby had switched out on her. As long as Tristan was there, Baby felt that Tristan could keep some boundaries on Joslyn's behalf because she wouldn't be so demanding, but the moment Tristan was away, Baby didn't want to play anymore. Joslyn started to feel used and downright hurt by all of these events. She couldn't understand what was going on here.

She knew that Baby was married as was she, but he said that he loved her. How can a man love her and not want to spend time with her, she thought? This started to remind Joslyn of the many lonely nights that Tristan had left her lying in bed wanting him to be with her and to stay with her and he so often refused because he had his gambling to do. Joslyn would often tell Tristan that the day would come when he would wish that he spent that quality time with her. Tristan never cared about those kinds of comments from Joslyn because he felt that he had everything under control; that is until he was arrested for passing counterfeit money through a bank in Ozark.

Tristan had been taken into custody in Ozark and needed Joslyn to drive more than an hour to bail him out. When Joslyn received the message from a close friend of Tristan's of his whereabouts and the cost, she flat out refused to go and pick him up. Joslyn had such vengeance in her towards Tristan that she didn't care what happened to him. Her thoughts were he should call his mom to come and get him or one of those women that he would so conveniently be with day in and day out.

She would not go and that was that. Tristan would call over and over again and Joslyn refused his calls and sent a message telling him that she knew that he would meet the day that he wished he would have spent quality time with her and respected her, because now that he needed her, she would never be that wife that he was in search of in his time of distress.

Tristan's mom came to his rescue as she had so many times before. Joslyn reflected on the times that she and Tristan had decided to get a divorce and his mom would beat them to their prospective attorney to pay the retainer fee before they had time to sign any papers.

This would always annoy Joslyn because after all, their marriage was none of her business, but she made it a priority in her life. Therefore, Joslyn would cancel going to the attorney just so his mom could lose her money and she could win this particular game as well. Joslyn knew that Tristan's family didn't feel that she was best suited for him in the first place, that's why when they got married no one knew. Tristan had decided to take her to the Justice of the

Peace and take care of this matter because it would cause major drama had he not.

Tristan was finally out of jail and living with his mom in New Brockton. He tried to get Joslyn to come visit many of times, but she refused because it appeared that he was allowing his mom to control yet another situation. Tristan went to his mom's because the heat was on him in Elba and the other surrounding cities because of his dealings with counterfeit money. Therefore, Tristan spent several months with his mom until he decided that he wanted to come back to Elba.

Tristan's mom decided that it would be best if he had his own place and not return to the apartment that he and Joslyn shared. At this point, Joslyn was really over all the drama with Tristan, his mom, his women, and Baby. She was so tired of all the lies, cheating, and hurting that she had been experiencing over the past years, months, and days. Joslyn just needed to be free of it all. She needed to find some sense of peace in her life as it seemed to be spiraling out of control.

After Tristan was settled into his place, he wanted Joslyn to come over so they could talk. Joslyn knew that in her head the relationship was over, but her heart kept saying "let's just see where this whole marriage is headed".

Around seven that evening, Joslyn decided to go and visit with Tristan to talk. When she knocked on the door his mom answered the door without so much as a hello and went and sat back down in the recliner and continued watching The Family Feud. Joslyn thought this to be quite odd, because why would his mom be at his place on a Saturday evening and why would he invite her over knowing that his mom was still there?

Joslyn took a seat on the sofa and waited for Tristan to come from the back of the apartment. While sitting there, Mrs. Carter never gave Joslyn even a glance or any indication that she wanted to have a conversation with her. Joslyn couldn't understand why she was so bitter towards her but knew one thing, that the feeling was mutual. Tristan came around the corner to the living room and summoned Joslyn to come to the entrance of the kitchen. When she made it to the entrance of the kitchen she asked how long his mom was there and how long had she planned to be there and Tristan said that she was just leaving.

Tristan and Joslyn sat at the breakfast nook and had a cup of tea while talking about superficial things waiting for Mrs. Carter to leave before discussing the concerns of their marriage. Time was ticking away as it was now eleven o'clock and Mrs. Carter had not so much as moved an eyebrow. It appeared to Joslyn that she was staying there because she didn't want her to stay over. After talking to Tristan a few more minutes, Joslyn decided that she would leave because it was very obvious that Mrs. Carter had planned to stay the night or just stay until she left.

After leaving Tristan and Mrs. Carter at his place, Joslyn decided to stop by the local bowling alley and see who was hanging out. She saw many acquaintances as well as Gabe Roundtree. Gabe was an old high school friend that she knew always had a thing for her. She noticed him because he was tall like she liked them, strongly built, and had a great sense of humor. Gabe was the life of the room and when she entered she took note of him right away. When she walked in, immediately Gabe noticed her newly fit and curvy assets as well.

He had always been intrigued with her, but she would never give him the time of day because she was always with Tristan and wasn't that type of woman then. However, the game had changed and so had Joslyn. Gabe was a well-known Contractor and Architect in Coffee County and abroad. He owned many businesses and had really become very successful over the years.

Joslyn would often hear of his many accomplishments and would marvel at how well he did for himself coming from a small town like Elba. Joslyn and Gabe spent quite a few hours during that night talking about old high school times and dreams that they had back then. It was such a breath of fresh air to be able to sit and talk with a man that really appeared to be interested in what she had to say, Joslyn thought to herself. She and Gabe concluded their conversation with exchanging numbers and Joslyn called it a night.

The next morning, Tristan called Joslyn and apologized for his mom's behavior and asked if he could spend some time with her that evening. Although, Joslyn had seemingly new interest in Gabe, she went because she still had some love for Tristan in her heart even though she knew he wasn't right for her. Tristan had prepared dinner and cocktails for the two of them.

The Filet Mignon, baked sweet potato, and broccoli was tender, sweet and mouthwatering. The cocktails consisted of the best Ice Tea in Coffee County. Tristan could always make the best ice tea especially when he put brown sugar and honey in it to taste. The dinner and conversation went well and Joslyn was feeling all sorts of mixed emotions concerning their relationship.

She knew that he wanted to be intimate with her but something inside of her had so many reservations about it. As the night progressed, Joslyn decided that Tristan was still her husband and that she would try once again to make it work.

After cleaning the kitchen, Joslyn and Tristan prepared for bed and the night was very blissful. Joslyn thought as she lay there wide awake and Tristan snoring very loudly next to her, that this would be a new beginning. Even though Joslyn had heard about the many escapades that Tristan had been having with many different women since moving into that apartment, she felt that they could overcome all of it.

As Joslyn was lying there she began to think about all the things that she had been hearing about Tristan and even though a moment before she felt that they could overcome them, she now came to a place of curiosity. Joslyn had heard that Tristan had made videos of himself and several of the women that he was with in Coffee County and abroad.

She was curious as to where these videos would be. As Tristan lay there sound asleep, Joslyn decided that she would satisfy her curiosity by searching for those videos. Low and behold under a pile of dirty laundry in the washroom, there it was, staring Joslyn in the face, the camcorder.

Joslyn knew that if he took the time to hide the camcorder under dirty laundry that there must be something to hide. As Joslyn loaded the tapes that she'd found in the dryer into the camcorder, she viewed Tristan doing all sorts of things with all sorts of women. They were of different shapes, sizes, color and socioeconomic backgrounds. Joslyn was appalled that she had allowed herself to be pulled into Tristan's web again, but that was about to end this very moment.

Joslyn got her things and ran down stairs with the tapes in hand as evidence that he was unfaithful to her. As Joslyn reached her car, Tristan had awakened and ran down stairs and asked for the tapes. Tristan had no idea that Joslyn had already viewed the evidence that would be a part of their subsequent divorce.

Tristan tried to convince Joslyn that the tapes consisted of football and other events like family reunions and things of that nature. When Joslyn assured Tristan that she knew what was on the tapes and proceeded to tell him, she and Tristan began to tussle over the tapes and as a result they were destroyed. Joslyn knew at that moment that it was truly over with her and Tristan.

She could never be with a man that totally had no regard for the vows he had taken with her. Even though, she made mistakes and had broken their vows as well,

Joslyn felt that it was all Tristan's fault. If he had given her the love that she deserved, then she would have never searched for love in all the wrong places trying to fill the void of him. It was finally settled they would get a divorce and move on with their lives.

CHAPTER EIGHT

"Baby on Deck"

*a*fter several weeks of waiting for the divorce to become finalized, Joslyn had already begun dating Gabe. She would occasionally see Baby from time to time because that was just the nature of the game that she was accustomed to playing. Joslyn really wanted to be loved and made so many mistakes as a result of seeking for that love. She began dating Gabe knowing that he really wasn't any better than what she had already experience, but her mentality of the game had shifted to a new level now. Joslyn was in a place of denial about what part she was playing in all the drama that was around her. She blamed Tristan for all the women that he was with and how he disrespected her.

She blamed Baby for not revealing to her about his wife and kids, even though she never asked. Moreover, she blamed the older women in her neighborhood for putting up with all the crap that the men would put them through as they stayed in those infectious relationships, while young girls like her looked on. Joslyn placed a lot of the blame on others because her thoughts were that a winner could never be at fault for any mishaps in their life, it had to be something or someone else's fault.

Joslyn worked many hours at Neiman's in Enterprise. She would work the morning shift most days because she had so many things going on in her personal life that the night shift would just cramp her style. Joslyn would work during the day and hang out with friends most evening. Joslyn was doing this so much that she didn't realize the toll it was taking on her. Joslyn started to feel ill with flu like symptoms.

Every day after work, Joslyn would go home and lie down because she truly felt that she had the flu or something. She was very weak, had chills on and off and would feel very feverish. Karen, the store manager at Neiman's noticed that Joslyn was looking a little pale and suggested that she take off work and go to the doctor to get checked out. Joslyn was a little apprehensive about going because she felt that is was a little bug and in a couple of days she would be fine.

However, later that afternoon, Joslyn began to experience what one would call a sick stomach. She felt as if she wanted to throw up, but Joslyn wasn't about to let that happen at work as she always viewed it as the most disgusting thing. So, Joslyn gave in and went to the Centre Care facility located at the end of the strip mall where she

It Was All a Game Until...

worked. Joslyn entered the office and signed in as a walk in patient and waited to be called in the back.

Once Joslyn was called back about 15 minutes later, she was asked why she was there. Joslyn explained her symptoms and told the physician of her flu theory. The physician asked her to urinate in a cup for a pregnancy test as a precautionary measure since she hadn't noticed that she hadn't had her cycle that month. Joslyn soon learned that her flu like symptoms weren't symptoms of the flu at all. Joslyn had just learned that she had a baby on deck.

Joslyn was at a loss for words as she couldn't understand how this happened, not to mention with whom it happened. Joslyn quickly reflected on the fact that her and Tristan's divorce wasn't final yet and the fact that she had already begun dating Gabe and everything that went along with that.

Joslyn didn't know what to think or do for that matter. She had to tell Tristan and Gabe about the situation. She especially had to tell Tristan because the following week they would be meeting with the Judge for the final hearing for their divorce and this could be a major hindrance in the judge granting the divorce. Tristan and Joslyn decided that they would not mention the pregnancy and their divorce was granted. Joslyn was now a pregnant divorcee with very little money and a mediocre job.

After the hearing for her divorce, Joslyn told Gabe of the situation and told him that she wasn't sure if the child was his or Tristan. She was pretty sure that it wasn't Tristan's as she had been with him more than nine years and had never become pregnant again since the termination of the pregnancy while they were dating.

However, she also thought that it could be a way of God trying to keep her and Tristan together by bringing a child into the marriage. Either way, Joslyn wasn't sure which of these two men would be her child's father, but she was certain of one thing. She was sure that she would be both parents to her child if need be because she knew that this was God's gift to her.

Joslyn became very ill while pregnant and could no longer work, so she moved out of her apartment and moved back home with her mother. This move made sense at the time because Joslyn was really scared and everything came with such uncertainty. For the next several months, Joslyn would eat, sleep, and eat again.

She was gaining weight rapidly and was very annoyed with the situation that she found herself in. Tristan was being with so many women and Gabe was back being with his son's mother. Although, he lied and said that they were no longer together and that's why Joslyn spent time with him in the first place. Joslyn had come to realize that she and her baby that was due to be born in another three months would make the best of their lives without either Tristan or Gabe.

On January 10, 1996, Jayla Carter was born into the world at Medical Center Enterprise weighing in at 8 pounds and 4 ounces. Jayla was most beautiful thing that Joslyn had ever seen. It just seemed so surreal that she was holding a baby that was her own. Joslyn was in awe every time Jayla would cry or make those little quilling like noises. She immediately loved this child so much. Joslyn knew that she wanted to be the best mom possible for her child even if neither Tristan nor Gabe stepped up to the plate.

Gabe stepped up to plate and began to provide for Jayla even though we hadn't confirmed that he was indeed Jayla's father. Tristan had no interest at all and made it perfectly clear that Jayla was not his daughter. Tristan went as far as to request a blood test for her because he refused to do what Gabe was doing without knowing. Joslyn was really irritated with Tristan because she had planned on having a blood test done herself, but he had the nerve to get his mom to call in a favor from one her friends at the blood bank to have this done as soon as possible.

Joslyn went down to the blood bank with Jayla a few weeks later and was tested. She asked if she could have Gabe come along too so we could settle this once and for all and they agreed. Several weeks later, a private number was calling Joslyn's phone. She would normally not answer private calls because she knew it would be one of Tristan's women that were being silly or she was afraid that Baby's wife would find her number out and call her. Despite her rules about private calls, Joslyn answered the phone and it was a technician from the blood blank with the results of their blood test.

When the technician gave her the news, Joslyn wasn't surprised at all because she was already certain of who Jayla's dad was months ago. Gabe was 99.99 percent Jayla's father. Joslyn was finally relieved to have documentation of who Jayla's dad was and now the smog that clouded her mind so many months prior was gone.

CHAPTER NINE

"Games, Games and More Games"

*J*oslyn had her daughter and now her life was headed in a totally different direction. She knew that Gabe had a son and was still being with his mom and probably several others considering that he traveled a lot. Not to mention that he was still seeing Joslyn quite often. Joslyn had to get herself together so she could be sure that Jayla had all that she needed and wanted. Gabe was now paying a substantial amount in child support in which could help with her bills, so Joslyn decided to go back to college and finish the degree that she started years ago.

Joslyn started school several months later and Gabe decided that he would marry his son's mother. Although, Joslyn wasn't in love with Gabe she felt a sense of loss in this particular situation because she and Gabe were seeing each other all along until a few days before he was to marry. Joslyn was shocked about this announcement as he had never let on that he was getting married. Joslyn knew that Gabe's son's mom would gloat about the fact that she married him and that she didn't because she had that same game winning mentality. Just as Joslyn had with Tristan, Gabe's baby mama was the same. She didn't care what was happening as long as she felt as if she was the winner. Joslyn knew this was the case so she accepted it and decided that she would move on.

    Joslyn decided to go back to work and continued to go to school to make a better life for her and her daughter. After Gabe came back from his honey moon, he came by alone to check on Jayla to see how things were going. Joslyn was a bit upset at the fact that he didn't value her enough to tell her what he was planning when he decided to marry. Gabe explained that he was somewhat forced into it because he was told that he would never see his son again.

Joslyn and Gabe sat and talked about what had happened and found themselves embracing each other yet again while their daughter lay napping in her crib. Joslyn and Gabe spent hours being intimate and the reality of his situation never once entered into her thoughts as she allowed him in her world once again.

    Joslyn was now laying next to yet another married man, gloating about how she was winning this situation. Gabe sat up just as Joslyn was playing this out in her head and announced that he had to go home. It was in that moment that Joslyn realize that she was being the other woman once again. Joslyn truly didn't care at this moment because she was not any one's wife and his son's mom deserved whatever competition that she got. Joslyn felt that forcing a man to marry her with threats, just to hold on to him., was just a part of the game.

By the time Jayla was 6 months old, Gabe and his wife had called it quits. Joslyn knew that it wouldn't last because of the way it came about. Joslyn began seeing more and more of Gabe but she also would still see Baby too if she wanted to. Joslyn had become a woman that did what she wanted with whom she wanted to do it with.

However, she would never allow her daughter to see or be connected with any of her indiscretions. She was very protective of her and wanted her life to be filled with the wonderful things that life had to offer. She knew that she would instill all the Christian values and morals in her life and would try to the best of her ability to demonstrate that lifestyle in front of her.

Gabe ended up going back on the road and of course that meant he would be seeing the many women that he was dating in all the different cities that he frequented. Joslyn decided that she wouldn't put all her energy into Gabe because it was clearly not the right thing to do as he was definitely not husband material.

Gabe was still out of town when he called to tell Joslyn that he was on his way back and wanted to see her and Joslyn knowing that she had made plans with yet another man she met at school, told him that he needed to call her once he got in town. Joslyn's new game was to do to men what they had so often did to women. She would be with whom she wanted according to her terms and nothing else.

As Gabe reach the state line in Dothan, Alabama, he called to say that he was coming over, Joslyn refused to answer because she didn't want it to be convenient for Gabe to come and go as he pleased.

Gabe called and called again and Joslyn still didn't answer. Gabe decided to go home and Joslyn decided that she would go to bed. Jayla was with Joslyn's mom because she had to work a double the next day. Around four in the morning Joslyn decided that she would go over to Gabe's house unannounced and spend the rest of the breaking dawn cuddling him.

When she arrived, she noticed an unfamiliar car in his drive way. Joslyn knew right then that since she didn't answer her phone that Gabe did what most men would do, he called another one of the women that he was involved with. Joslyn was a bit upset because she thought that the game that she played earlier last night by not answering would have Gabe wondering what she was up too, but instead it made him do what he was accustomed to doing.

Gabe was also a womanizer and the women that he became involved with knew this but still gave him the time of day, even Joslyn. He really was incapable of truly loving anyone and it was just foolish for any of the women including her to think otherwise. Joslyn knew that she had to leave Gabe alone because this game wasn't at all what it was cracked up to be. Actually, it was taking too much energy out of her because she was always putting things on hold or her friends off and even turning down dates that were potentially good husband prospects for a man that wasn't worth her time.

Joslyn decided that Gabe would be a thing of the past. She also decided that Baby would be put into that category too because she had just learned that he was cheating on her and his wife with another woman. Joslyn knew that she had to take her game of winning elsewhere and a little more seriously.

It Was All a Game Until...

CHAPTER TEN

"Losing Becomes a Reality"

*J*oslyn was making things happen. She had finally worked hard and finished college and was well on her way to making a remarkable life for her and her daughter. However, there was one thing that was missing from this equation; she didn't have a man in her life and winning seemed so unorthodox now. Joslyn majored in psychology and she had landed a job in Enterprise at the local family counseling agency that helps families deal with their issues. Week after week she would speak with men, women and children about their issues and try to help them process what was happening in their lives.

Many times Joslyn would speak with a woman or young girl that had experienced the same things as she, but she never saw herself losing or really broken from any of it. She deemed herself as winner because no matter what was happening she was in control and after all, winners could never be at fault for the mishaps in their lives.

As Joslyn counseled different women throughout the week, she started to see herself in many of them. She was really floored when this woman came in all distraught because she could never find a man that didn't have someone already. Joslyn could identify with this totally because as of late every single man that she dated or that took an interest in her was in a relationship with someone else.

He would either be married, living with his girlfriend or lie and say that he was single when he was in fact seeing someone. Joslyn spoke with this woman and wanted to get to the bottom of why she was allowing these types of men in her life. The woman couldn't answer that question, she could only say that it satisfied her at the time it was happening, but now she's starting to feel used and mishandled.

As Joslyn listened she noticed that she was a picture perfect image of what the woman had described in her. After Gabe, Joslyn had been dating man after man. Each one of these men came with their story about what happened in their relationship and why they are not with the last girlfriend, baby mama or wife. Joslyn would take what was being told to her and try to fill the void that each of these men said that their previous relationship didn't fulfill.

Joslyn's behavior was much like that of a man at this point. Men would always listen to what a woman had to say about what is going on in their lives and then used that information to get what they wanted from these women. Joslyn was no different. She would get involved with these men and believe within her psyche that she was winning and in control of her situations.

While Joslyn would counsel these women she was actually counseling herself as well. She would never let on to anyone that she had learned so much about herself while listening to other women talk about themselves. She could never understand why she attracted the same kind of man each and every time. She could never understand why the excitement and high that she normally got from winning was no longer present.

She often wondered how she got to this place in her life. Joslyn had come to realize that she was never winning at all. She had finally come to the realization that all these years she was losing. She was losing because she thought she was in control and that the men she was choosing were men of her choice only to find out that those men where choosing her.

She would always question herself about the men that she would get involved with. She felt like she had "SEEKING MAN THAT IS INVOLVED WITH SOMEONE ELSE" on her forehead because that is what she attracted. Joslyn never thought about the energy that she was sending into the universe. She never considered that the law of attraction played a huge role in her life. Joslyn was a woman that had to win at all cost regardless of the circumstances, and the men that she attracted had that same mind set. Joslyn never once thought about how valuable she was. Even though she told her clients about their value and how valid they were in each of their own world, she had never grasped that herself.

She never valued herself enough to the point where she demanded the respect of a man. Joslyn had allowed Tristan to come into her life and blindside her into marrying him by taking her down to the Justice of the Peace and she had no idea what was happening until she got there.

She went through a life of hell with him because he was constantly cheating, verbally abusing, sexually abusing, and mentally abusing her and she decided to stay with him during, and after all of the abuse because she didn't want to lose. But, lose what? She allowed Baby to use her by taking what she shared with him about her husband to his advantage.

He was very smooth, said all the right things and made her feel like she was best thing since sliced bread all while he knew he wasn't going to leave his wife and kids. She allowed Gabe to come back and forth into her life so many times because he was her daughter's father. She had dated this man and that man all with the same M.O. and thought that she was the master game player and winner in all of it.

Subsequently, Joslyn had finally gotten the big picture of the winner that she had portrayed herself to be and that winner was actually a loser. Joslyn had played so many games and made so many bad choices that it never dawned on her that she was the biggest loser of them all. She did not like who she had become and at this point in her life she knew that knowing that she was a loser, her life would definitely have to change.

Day after day she would hear these same kind of stories. Woman gets with man, she falls for him, and she allows him to cheat on her, beat on her, and totally disrespect her all because she was trying to prove a point to someone.

Elaine was the last client of the day because she was a new client; but, by the time this session was over, Joslyn felt like she was her only client all day because she was physically drained and hyperventilating. Joslyn introduced herself and asked Elaine to have a seat. Before Joslyn could get settled in and get her materials out, she started to cry. It caught Joslyn a little off guard because usually the tears came during the session and not during the greeting period. Joslyn stop gathering her things and ask her to tell her what was going on and she wiped her tears and began.

She started by saying she had been married to her husband Dexter for more than ten years and he has never truly acknowledge her and the commitment of their marriage. Joslyn asked her why does she feel that way and she began by saying because he would always cheat on me and dismiss me when I would say anything to him about his behavior. He is not only selfish in this marriage, he just does not care. Joslyn instructed her to go on and explain what she means. She started again and said," that her husband had cheated on her with several of her so called friends and had been intimate with them in their home. He has been accused of getting several women pregnant, and when I asked him about the situation, he would deny it only to find out later that it was true.

He would come home late and sometimes not at all with a woman's fragrance and lipstick all over him; he would basically rape me whenever I refused to be intimate with him. He would take a knife or something sharp and cut my undergarments off and force me to be with him. He doesn't want me with my family much because my sisters would always come and tell me what they saw him doing.

He would go out and get mad at the woman that he was seeing and come home and take it out on me. One time, he was so mad at the woman he was seeing that he came home and I was sitting on the couch reading. He walked in and went straight to our bedroom. A few moments later, he asked me to come here, and I didn't want to be bothered, so I refused. He yelled for me again and I went in to see what he wanted. As I reached the room where he was, he began slapping me and shoving me around and I had no idea why this was happening.

I started to scream and he started to choke me. He then threw me on the bed, cut the lights off, and I heard him putting bullets in his gun. While he was loading his gun, he was saying that he was done and that he should just kill me. I was so afraid that I just whimpered because I didn't want to say or do anything that would trigger him and make him go through with what he had just said. As I lay there in the dark, I could remember the one scripture that my grandmother would say often and that was Psalm 23.

I began saying it in my head, The Lord is my Shepard, I shall not want, He makes me lie down in green pastures, He leads me beside the still waters, He restores my soul, he leads in the paths of righteousness for His name sake, yea though I walk through the valley of the shadow of death, I will fear no evil because Thou are with me. The moment those words were released in my mind "because Thou are with me", Dexter jump up and left the apartment. I didn't see him for days and I was actually relieved.

I never shared any of this with my family because I didn't want them to turn against him. She looked at Joslyn and said, "I know you are wondering why I stayed with him after all that has happened in this marriage". Joslyn was speechless because by this point she was having trouble breathing, but she couldn't allow her patient to take note of that. Therefore, she was able to muster up enough breath to say, "Why have you stayed?"

Elaine proceeded to tell her that she stayed because she didn't want to be a failure, she didn't want any of those women he was with to have him and she would never have any woman say that she took him from her. Joslyn then asked her," now that you have said all of that, is there anything that you want to gain from meeting with me"?

Elaine told Joslyn that the one thing that she wanted to get from meeting with her was to learn how to love herself enough, just enough, to stop all the madness in her life. Joslyn pondered her statement for a moment and told her that they would definitely get to the bottom of why things are the way that they are in her life. She then told her that her time was up and they would start from where they left off next visit.

Joslyn was totally flabbergasted by the time she made it home from work. She didn't show any of the emotions that she was feeling in front of her client because she was supposed to be the one that gave the help, not the one that needed it. Joslyn sat on the edge of her bed reflecting on all that Elaine had said and began to weep.

Joslyn started to remember that Dexter and Tristan were one in the same. Although, they were two different men, they were the same as it relates to their behavior because most of what Elaine had described that Dexter had done to her in their marriage, Tristan had done the exact same thing.

The women, the raping, the fighting, the threatening to kill her, and the disrespect was so fresh in her mind as she sat weeping. Joslyn had finally got a release that very moment when she sat their crying because she had suppressed so much of what Tristan had done in their marriage. Joslyn was a very strong willed person and nothing got to her much or so she thought nothing got to her much until she began looking back over her life. She knew from this experience that she would never be the same again. She knew that she would forever be changed because those tears actually worked as a cleansing of all the suppressed unhappiness in her soul.

Joslyn returned to work the next day and resumed counseling women with the same story over and over again. Joslyn was so affected by all that she was hearing and by all that she had come to terms with about herself that she decided that she needed to request to take a sabbatical from work because it was really draining her.

It wasn't draining her in the sense that it was tiring, but it drained her in the sense of her emotions and how each and every time she heard a woman speak about their issues with men it would literally cause her physical illness. She had become so sad and weary about her life and how games had put her in such a state of resentment towards herself.

Joslyn knew that she had been exposed even if it was only to herself. She knew that no matter what she did from that moment on that she had to do in a way that was contrary to what she was accustomed to doing. But, how would she do that? She didn't know any other way to think or to handle life's situations other than with a winning attitude and mindset. Joslyn often would think about scriptures and how they were supposed to be a road map that would guide you along the way but she never really and truly gave them a chance to minister to her. She went to church Sunday after Sunday and took her daughter and did everything that a mother that was living by faith should have done in front of her daughter, but behind closed doors and out of her sight she had her own agenda.

Now, that she had come to the realization of whom she really was and what a mess she had made of her life, she knew that the scriptures would be the only thing that could bring her back to where God wanted her to be.

As she was off on her sabbatical, Joslyn decided to really take out time and read God's word for His guidance. She knew from attending church, that there was always healing in God's word if the individual surrendered to his will and his way. She heard story after story of His healing power and how He extended grace and mercy to each of us every day, so she decided that this was a great place to start the healing process.

Joslyn wanted so much to have a life that was good in the sight God. She also wanted others to see her in a different element. She felt that the choices that she had made in the past placed a stigma on her that left her feeling like the men in the bible that were plagued with leprosy and no one wanted to get near them.

Although, it wasn't as bad as that, she knew that many women classified her as a woman with no boundaries because of her demeanor when it came to what she was doing. Many women didn't know her personally, but because the men that she was with, girlfriend, baby mama, or wife was so unforgiving for what she had done, they would tell anyone that would listen about her. Joslyn never once blamed them for their feelings towards her because she was indeed the ruthless one when it came to winning. She didn't care who she hurt because it was ultimately about her. Joslyn realized at that moment that she was really hurting when she was with Tristan.

The fact that he could be with women that she thought were her friends and they could be with him, made her not think about anything, but getting revenge. She wanted other women to feel what she was feeling and no matter how many times she went down this road she never completely felt that great about what she was doing. After all, the women that she'd hurt hadn't really done anything to her.

Although she felt like Gabe's wife deserved what she got, she knew deep within herself that it wasn't the right thing to do to anyone. While Joslyn was evaluating the events in her life, she had another revelation, hurting people, hurt people. She had heard this saying many times before as well as used it in her practice, but she could never grasp the whole concept of it in her own life even though she was a counselor.

But, Joslyn knew that before she could really continue on with her practice as a psychologist that she had to really get it together. She could no longer counsel these women and she was one of them. She refused to keep up the façade that she put on with her clients and everyone around her. She had to change the way she looked at life and the games that she played.

CHAPTER ELEVEN

"Changing the Game"

*J*oslyn had been on her sabbatical for several weeks now trying to sort out her life. A couple of her co-workers agreed to take on her case load until she felt that she was ready to resume her practice. Joslyn never went into details with her co-workers or her boss about the reason she needed to take the time away, she just stated that she had some personal things that she needed to handle and it would be time consuming. This also gave her more time to spend with Jayla as she was growing up to be the most adorable little princess.

Joslyn often reflected on the last session she had with Elaine and how at that moment it caused her to look inside herself. As she reflected on that session, while sitting on her bed, the phone rang. It was her sister Terrell asking if she wanted to go to church with her. Joslyn had attended church, but this was a service with a Prophetess named Barbara Gaines from Orlando, Florida. She had heard so many wonderful things about the prophetess and to be quite honest was a little afraid to attend the service. She was afraid because she felt that she would be told some things about her life and she did not want to be exposed in a crowd of people at church, not to mention her sister but Joslyn agreed to go anyway.

The service started at 7:30 and her sister wanted to get there as early as possible because she never liked to sit in the back. Upon arriving around 7:15, the church was nearly full. Joslyn, Terrell and several cousins and friends all sat together in middle isle near the back of the church. The service hadn't started yet but the praise team was getting ready to come up and begin.

The service began promptly at 7:30 and everyone was standing and praising the Lord. The praise team sang for nearly 20 minutes or so and then Prophetess Gaines walked out onto the platform and began her message. She walked across the platform to and fro sharing the word of God. She was a powerhouse. She spoke with such authority and certainty that you could feel her anointing instantly when she spoke.

She was calling people out telling them what the Lord had spoken to her and many were getting the release and deliverance that they needed in that hour. It was obvious to Joslyn that so many people were hurting, whether it was physical, mental, financial, or spiritual, they were really struggling with some things.

About an hour had past and Prophetess Gaines continued to speak God's word when suddenly she called out for the lady in the back with the Yellow Dress to come up front. Everyone began to look around to see who she was speaking of. Joslyn even looked around for the lady in the yellow dress.

It hadn't dawned on her that she was wearing a yellow dress. As Joslyn was looking around for the individual, She made it clear of whom she was asking for. She called out Joslyn specifically by her dress, hair, and where she was sitting.

Joslyn was a little hesitant at first to move because she still wasn't sure if she meant her. Joslyn looked up at Prophetess Gaines as she pointed towards herself and she agreed that she was whom in which she wanted to come up front.

As Joslyn walked the isle making her way down to the front, she began to shake and sweat profusely. Joslyn feared that this would happen and was terrified. When she reached the point where Prophetess Gaines was standing, she immediately placed her hand on Joslyn's head and began to pray for her.

Joslyn was already in tears by then because she felt that this was nothing but God intervening on her behalf. She prayed in other tongues and then began to tell Joslyn what the spirit spoke to her. She told Joslyn that she had suffered a nervous breakdown and didn't even know it and that she had been through so much in her young life that many women would never experience. She continued by telling her how God has a plan for her life and that he would make all the crooked paths straight and give her, her heart's desire. She anointed Joslyn's head with oil and prayed fervently for her and at that moment the spirit came upon Joslyn and she was out of it.

When Joslyn came through, she was lying on the floor and her dress was soaked from all the tears. She was escorted back to her seat and the tears just continued to flow. When the service was over, Prophetess Gaines sent an usher over to Joslyn and asked if she would come so she could have a moment with her.

As Joslyn walked over to speak with Prophetess Gaines, she knew that something spectacular had just happened in her life. Prophetess Gaines just wanted to tell her that she was going to make it and that God had plans for her and to keep walking in belief of that.

She then gave her a hug and Joslyn and her sister left to go get something to eat. While eating their meal, they talked about the service and about what Prophetess Gaines had shared with her. Joslyn had never shared all the things that she had done or gone through with her family because she was very private in that sense.

However, she did tell her sister that Prophetess Gaines was referring to all that she had endured with Tristan. They continue talking quite a bit about this and then that all while finishing their meal and afterwards went home.

The next day when Joslyn woke up, she felt something quite different. She didn't feel the heaviness anymore about her clients or her life. The heaviness that had consumed her for weeks now was no longer there and Joslyn found herself questioning why? She reminisced about the service the night before and felt for the first time that God could possibly hear her cry.

Joslyn had prayed about many things, many times but felt like her prayers weren't being answered because of what she had done or was doing. But even though she had done so many things wrong, she still questioned why they weren't being answered at the time because the bible says that God's promises are Yea and Amen in 2 Corinthians 1:20. Moreover, it says, "For I know the plans I have for you," declares the LORD, "plans to prosper you and not to harm you, plans to give you hope and a future in Jeremiah 29:11.

So, in knowing what the bible says when it came to God's promises, Joslyn still couldn't comprehend that she had a part to do in order for His promises to be Yea and Amen and for the plans that He has for her to manifest themselves into her life.

Days past and Joslyn could not get the service out of her mind nor the scriptures about God's promises and plans towards her. She knew that she had made so many mistakes and although she had asked for forgiveness, she had not truly forgiven herself. She didn't know how to do that. She was so resentful towards herself and all that she had done, that she really thought that going to God and asking Him for anything would really be out of the question. Joslyn would replay every single incident and indiscretion in her mind convincing herself that she was not worthy of His promises nor plans either for that matter. She desired a husband for her and a father for her daughter. She wanted a family more than anything.

Anytime, she thought about praying for this husband and father, she would get this unsettling feeling inside of her that spoke to her saying, "yeah right"! It had gotten to the point that Joslyn downright refused to pray for that anymore because she couldn't stand the feeling that she would have first off and secondly, she felt that she wasn't worthy of neither.

Although, the bible spoke of her worth, and how God loved her, she still struggled with praying for something as simple as a husband and father. Joslyn thought about how a God of love and promises could even consider giving her the desires of her heart when she so randomly intruded in someone else's marriage, or relationship. She was so full of herself and the games that she played that she never took anyone else into consideration, but herself. But now that the revelation of who she had become had emerged so forcefully to her attention, she had to deal with the Joslyn that was now broken.

Joslyn was so broken hearted and it wasn't because of a man. It was because she was not a good person in her eyesight. Yes, she was good to her family and friends. She would help them in whatever capacity that she could, but that wasn't enough. Being good in the way of giving, comforting, and, or supporting her family and friends just wasn't the good that she desired in her mess of a life. She wanted to feel good about the future choices that she made. She wanted to feel good about being a respectful person, who not only respected who she was as a woman but respected other women in the same manner.

As Joslyn was thinking this, it dawned on her, that many women don't truly respect other women. It is the same for men, but women differed because she would go out of her way to gain whatever attention she got from a man and it didn't matter if he was married or not, as long as it satisfied that winning spirit within her. Joslyn knew this to be a fact because she had played this game of winning for so long that she really didn't know any other way to be.

As time went on, Joslyn was trying to get herself together. She went to church a lot more, even to the mid-week bible service, trying to figure out her messy life. She would often talk with the mothers of the church asking questions about being redeemed and delivered from the strongholds of your past and about forgiveness as well as how does a person learn to forgive themselves?

Mother Maxi was the main person that Joslyn spoke too because she had known her since she was a little girl. Joslyn was sure that back in the day, when she was living on Compton Circle as a little girl, that Mother Maxi was one of her dad's honeys. Although, she never saw him with her or anything, there were always rumors about them and what was going on. Not to mention, that she took special interest in his kids and brought them gifts for holidays and birthdays. Mother Maxi was the greatest. Whenever Joslyn was going through life's obstacles, she could always call on her to be a leaning post.

Joslyn's mother was always there for her as well, but when it came to issues that concerned her indiscretions she couldn't talk to her mom about that. Now that Joslyn was in a place of brokenness, she had to talk to Mother Maxi because she knew that she would keep it real and tell her what she wanted and needed her to know, rather than what Joslyn wanted to hear.

She began by saying, "that no matter what you have done Joslyn; God can forgive you and heal you". She went on to say "that once he has forgiven you, it is thought about no more. He is unlike man that remembers every single act that is committed against Him".

She explained again how God's love for us is unconditional and that no matter what we do, it doesn't stop Him from loving us. Joslyn began to cry as Mother continued to speak to her. She cried because the thought of having someone love you and you feel that you are so undeserving was truly overwhelming for her to totally get that in her spirit.

Joslyn continued to cry as Mother began to pray with her and asked God for His healing power to fall upon her and to grant her the desires of her heart. Mother was a prayer warrior and Joslyn knew that if anyone could get a message to God it would be Mother. Joslyn told Mother that she received every single thing that she said and that she would stand on those prayer requests and believe and trust that God would do just that.

Joslyn was so in awe by the presence of God. When mother was praying, she could feel the joy and calmness of God's spirit and it made her want to run as fast as she could. Now that she was reminiscing about it, it made her feel that a run wasn't a bad idea. So Joslyn began to run down the street, around the corner and over to the adjacent neighborhood and back. While she was running, she could hear Mother's voice saying God loves you; God loves you, over and over again. Joslyn began saying it too, God loves me; God loves me!

By the time she finished her run, she had really come to terms with God loving her. She was a new person in Christ and wanted to do all she could to hold on to what she had in Him. Joslyn realized that through His love and compassion for her, God allowed His Son Jesus to go to the Cross and suffer for her sins. That was enough right there to allow Joslyn to know that the game had finally changed and that she needed to reconstruct and redirect her way of thinking about the game and how it should be played.

It Was All a Game Until...

CHAPTER TWELVE

"The Reconstruction"

The sun was shining through Joslyn's sheer black curtains in her bedroom quite earlier than normal the next morning. It was Saturday and Joslyn had planned to sleep in and relax as Jayla was with her aunt. Many weekends, Jayla would stay with her aunt because there were always a lot of kids in that neighborhood for her to play with. As Joslyn lay their contemplating on whether to get out of bed or not, there was a knock on her door. Joslyn couldn't figure out who would come to her place unannounced. As she slipped on her purple velvet robe and black Donna Karen slippers, the knock became persistent.

Joslyn yelled at the person knocking that she would be there in a moment. The person continued to knock as Joslyn swung her door open and asked what your problem is? Just as the words were coming out of her mouth she noticed that the man at the door was Gabe Round Tree, Jayla's dad. She stood there for a moment trying to figure out what made him show up after all this time. Gabe had been gone for months since the demise of his marriage and she was sure that she had heard that he was getting ready to marry someone else. Therefore, she could not imagine what he wanted.

After the few moments of silence, Joslyn asked him in and offered him something to drink. Gabe didn't want anything to drink. He said that he just wanted to talk to her. She said okay and wanted to know about what. Gabe went on to explain his bad choices with getting married and being with this woman and that woman and that he was a changed man. He continued to say that he wanted a family with her and Jayla.

At that moment, Joslyn was floored. Immediately, that game mentality surfaced yet again. She started to think how much better she must be than all the other women that he was with because why else would he come back so strongly to get her. That way of thinking only lasted for a split second because Joslyn remember that she had heard that he was getting ready to marry someone else that she didn't know. She hesitated and then told Gabe that she was aware of his plans to marry and why would he be over to her place talking such foolishness.

Gabe was shocked that she knew about his plans and said that if she told him not to do it, he wouldn't. Joslyn couldn't believe what he was saying and stopped him in his tracks. Joslyn told him that she wasn't sure about what kind of game that he was trying to play but she wasn't going to be a part of any of it anymore. She told him that the only thing that they had in common was the support and love of their daughter and that she was definitely not the woman for him and then asked him to leave. Gabe stood there totally dumbfounded because this type of stunt always worked in the past with her.

But what he didn't know was that Joslyn had an experience with God and refused to resort back to the same person she was before. Gabe left and she was relieved. She was so proud that she had recognized the tactic that the devil was trying to use so he could go to God and say "I told you so".

She wasn't about to let that happen as it had so many times before. Not that she was living her life in a Christian manner, but the fact that so many times she had allowed herself to be pulled into a messy situation without clearly thinking about the ramifications of it.

Joslyn began to really get involved in church and its activities. She started working with the young girls in her community because she wanted to make an impact in their lives and give back. She was always great with talking with people, as this is why she chose a career in psychology. She was still on her sabbatical from work and needed something to keep her focused on her goal of healing herself and allowing God to work on her from the inside out.

It Was All a Game Until...

The young girls in the community were from many different types of homes. Some were in homes that had two parents; some were in single parent homes, while others were being reared by their grandparents. Joslyn wanted to focus on the many issues that she faced and the ones that she saw many of her friends were involved in. She started meeting with the young ladies twice a month to discuss matters of their hearts and those issues that most women faced at some point in their lives.

At first, the girls were really reserved and didn't want to open up and share much because they were afraid of her telling their parents and because she was an adult. Joslyn had to really get them to trust her by saying that what was spoken in their meeting would never be shared outside the confinement of the four walls of the room.

This made the girls a lot more confident and they began to open up. In particular, they opened up about relationships with their peers and their parents. Many felt that their parents didn't understand their issues and all their parent did was fuss and said "no" about everything. Joslyn had to start by telling them the many mistakes that she made in life concerning relationships.

She had to open up and really become so transparent with these young girls because they needed someone to be real with them and help them understand that it is okay to feel what you feel, but you have to channel those feelings in a positive way.

One meeting in particular, Joslyn shared with these young girls how allowing a boy to pressure you into doing something that you are not ready to do is wrong. She went on to tell them that doing it because you don't want Susie Q to have him is even more wrong.

Joslyn really felt the need to convey this message because that was a big part of the competition that she had played most of her life. She was determined not to let anyone say that they had taken or was with any one that she was with. She really didn't want any of these young girls to make any of the same mistakes that she had, thus sharing this part was imperative because she sensed that several of them were already headed down this road.

The girls opened up the discussion by asking "What should you do when you feel like you are being pressured to be intimate and you know that you really aren't ready?" Joslyn wanted to be clear when she told them that anytime a person tries to pressure you into anything that goes against what you believe or what you have been taught, that person does not have your best interest at heart. It really took some convincing before they really got the message, but by the end of the meeting, several of them were happy that they had that discussion.

The meetings with the girls continued as they would meet twice monthly on Mondays to have these discussion. The meetings were helping Joslyn more than she had recognized because it caused her to read her bible more and utilized what she taught the girls in her own life.

There were many scriptures that Joslyn had come across from her daily reading that were so profound that she had to share with her girls. Not only did she come across scriptures, but she came up with a motto for her girls that she hoped that they would remember and take in consideration when making choices in their lives.

The motto that she told them was "My life is a reflection of my conscious and subconscious choices; I must make a conscious effort to choose my path; when I do not choose consciously; my path becomes my default". Joslyn came up with this motto because it described her life in a nut shell.

She wanted the young girls to really understand that if you don't truly think about the choices that you are making and you make that choice for whatever reason; it is not anyone's fault but your own. She really wanted the young girls to understand that, you can't blame anyone for the bad choices that you make, but yourself.

Joslyn felt very good about working with these young ladies and really took it very seriously. She needed to do this because in a strange way it helped reconstruct her own way of thinking. When she was not taking care of Jayla and spending time with the young ladies that she was mentoring, Joslyn would read her bible and other books that she was either given or purchased. One book in particular that she had begun to read was "Single Whole and Holy" This book, she thought, was perfect. It described who she was now as it relates to her status of being single and it also set a precedence of where she wanted to be. She wanted so badly to be a different person than that of before.

She needed to be Whole and she definitely desired to live a life that was Holy and acceptable to God. Joslyn especially wanted to live a life that was acceptable to God and knew that being with someone and being intimate with them wasn't acceptable. After reading the scripture Romans 12:1-2, that says, *"I appeal to you therefore, brothers, by the mercies of God, to present your bodies as a living sacrifice, holy and acceptable to God, which is your spiritual worship. Do not be conformed to this world, but be transformed by the renewal of your mind, that by testing you may discern what is the will of God, what is good and acceptable and perfect"*.

Joslyn knew for a fact that restructuring her life to what this scripture was speaking to her was not an option. As she sat and read this, she began to weep yet again. What this scripture said to her was so profound as if Jesus just tapped her on her shoulders and said," After all I've done for you, the least you could do is treat your body as the temple that it is, that is the least you could do for me". This made her weep so uncontrollably that she didn't realize that she had cried herself to sleep until she was awaken by her alarm clock at 6:00am the next morning.

Joslyn still had the bible and her books lying next to her when she was awaken by the alarm clock. She got up and proceeded into to Jayla's room to get her dressed for school all while trying to decide what she would do the rest of the day. She didn't have any clients to see, she didn't have any girls to mentor or any errands to run. Therefore, after taking Jayla to school, she decided that she would go to the beach and sit in the sun and continue to read the book that was given to her earlier.

When she arrived at the beach, she took her blanket and found a quite shady spot under a palm tree near the edge of a fence by the playground area. That was a perfect spot because this time of day it was very quiet at the beach. The kids were at school and the parents that did have their kids there were the ones that had toddlers and infants that rarely made that much ruckus.

After getting all of her things settled in the shaded area, Joslyn retrieved her book from her bag, along with her bottled water and began reading. The book Single, Whole, and Holy had some really interesting points in it. In the book Joslyn noticed how life was constantly contradicting itself. One minute it says one thing to you and the next it says something else. It explained how we have two spirits warring against each other; one being the Spirit man and the other being the man of Flesh.

It strongly suggested that whatever spirit that is fed most is the one that often wins the raging battle within you. The apostle Paul in Romans 7:15 stated that *"For I do not understand my own actions, I am baffled, bewildered. I do not practice or accomplish what I wish, but I do the very thing that I loathe"*. This made perfect sense to Joslyn now because many times she would do things and then question herself about why she did what she had done.

Joslyn sat and pondered this for a moment and realized that she was nurturing the flesh part of her more than her spirit part. She remembers hearing so much as she was growing up about the spirit you feed the most will dominate your life, just as she had read moments ago.

She was now convinced that this had to be what was happening in her life all these years because she was more concerned about how she ended up in the end. Her feelings had nothing to do with God and whether her actions pleased Him or not, she was concerned about simply being pleased with her performance and winning in any given situation.

Joslyn sat for hours and continued reading; and as she read, she realized how she missed reading as she would read to cope when she was married to Tristan. Her thoughts were interrupted by her phone reading. Joslyn normally would put her phone on silent while reading because she hated being interrupted by anything while reading.

She decided that she wouldn't answer because she knew it couldn't be anything of any importance because Jayla was in school and she was still on her time off from work. The phone continued to ring back to back, so she decided to answer the phone. At first she didn't recognize the voice as it sounded really muffled in the phone.

When she said hello again, she noticed that it was Baby's voice. Joslyn became really annoyed that he was calling her phone. She had moved on from all the nonsense in her life and was trying to be and do better things. Nonetheless, she said hello and listened to what he had to say.

He wasn't really making any sense to her because he sounded intoxicated. She told him to speak slowly so she could understand what he was saying. He told her that he had separated from his wife and that he wanted to see her.

Joslyn was a little puzzled by this because at no time during this stage in her life did she want to be with him or anyone for that matter. She was trying to focus on getting herself together for her and her daughter and didn't want the baggage of any past relationship. Especially one that had a wife and children involved in it.

Joslyn tried to be as polite as possible and told Baby that she was sorry that things weren't working out for him and that she hope that things got better. He went on to say that they could be better if she accepted his proposal to be with him. The old Joslyn would have accepted because that would have meant that she won in the end because he came back to her, but the Joslyn that was trying to reconstruct her life was not about to have that.

She couldn't risk setting herself up for more hurt nor could she disappoint God any more than she had already. She told Baby that she couldn't do that and that she couldn't speak with him anymore. Baby became really irate with her stating that she was the cause of his marriage falling apart and that she misled him in this whole matter. He continued ranting and raving until finally she hung up her phone and blocked his number so he could never call again.

It was nearing the time to pick up Jayla from school so Joslyn gathered her things and began walking to her car. As she walked she reflected on what Baby had said about her being the cause of his marriage failing. Joslyn thought the nerve of him saying that.

She didn't make vows to his wife, she didn't live with her nor did she have kids with her or did she force him to spend time with her, so how could she be at fault. The moment she spoke those words, "how could she be at fault", Joslyn realized that she was indeed at fault. She played a part in the relationship with him and she caused another woman to hurt because of her decision to win, but win at what?

Joslyn was once again feeling resentful towards herself as she drove to pick up Jayla. When she arrived home, she prepared dinner, helped Jayla with homework and put her to bed. After getting herself prepared for bed, Joslyn reflecting on what Baby had said again. She felt awful that his marriage was falling apart and felt even worse knowing that she played a role in that. Why did she allow what Tristan was taking her through to cause her to hurt someone else? She realized that the game mentality had hurt her and the statement "if you can't beat them join them" how this way of thinking has destroyed someone else's life. She knew that all the choices that she made was her own fault, and that it wasn't Baby's wife and children's fault that a woman would intrude in their lives and be a contributing factor in a failed marriage and broken home.

The more she thought about this, the more she felt that she needed to do something. She had no idea of what to do in this situation. Therefore, she took her bible out and proceeded to read whatever she flipped the bible open too. She had been reading a lot in the book of Romans so there was a book mark in that book, so when the bible flipped open it was no surprise that it landed in Romans, but on another chapter.

It landed on Romans 8. Romans 8:1-4 says, *"Therefore, there is now no condemnation for those who are in Christ Jesus, because through Christ Jesus the law of the Spirit who gives life has set you[a] free from the law of sin and death. For what the law was powerless to do because it was weakened by the flesh, [b] God did by sending his own Son in the likeness of sinful flesh to be a sin offering.[c] And so he condemned sin in the flesh, in order that the righteous requirement of the law might be fully met in us, who do not live according to the flesh but according to the Spirit.*

Upon reading this, Joslyn was able to really understand what she had already read and learned growing up as a child. She learned that Jesus went to the cross barring all our sins and we can't be condemned anymore if we are in Christ Jesus. She knew that there was nothing physically she could do for Baby and his marriage but spiritually she could go to God repent and ask for forgiveness for what she had done concerning this matter and all matters that she hadn't repented for. She had to start there because everything else that she desired to do in an effort to reconstruct her life would be meaningless if she didn't start there.

It Was All a Game Until...

CHAPTER THIRTEEN

"God Delivers"

Year after year, month after month, and day by day, Joslyn continued to seek God's redeeming face to reconstruct her way of thinking. Jayla had grown up so fast and was playing basketball in middle school. Her grades were outstanding and she was very respectful and was becoming very responsible with her studies and her chores. She and Joslyn had really made a great life together; not only as mother and daughter but also as good pals.

Joslyn had gone back to work a year or so earlier and had made remarkable progress with her own issues and demons. She had really grown and started to get the fever to want a husband again and a father for Jayla. Many times in the past she would seek to find this wonderful man that she wanted as a husband and father for Jayla. Although, Jayla had a biological father, she didn't have a father in the home and Joslyn really wanted that for her daughter. Most times when she dated, that was the goal that she had in mind. It didn't matter what else was happening with the man, as long as he was a prospect to fit the bill of being husband and father. In hindsight, Joslyn realized that none of the men that she dated, including Jayla's dad, were equipped with the right tools to fulfill the role of either. They were just a part of the game that she played and not very well.

Joslyn was so convinced that she was ready to fulfill the role of wife that she started to share that belief with many of her friends. She would tell them that she was going to get married within the next year; although, she wasn't dating nor did she have any one in mind. She just knew that she wanted to have a family for her and her daughter. She remembered one night in bible study that the lesson discussed was "Speak the Word".

The teacher of the lesson talked about how there is life and death in the power of your tongue using Proverbs 18:21. She went on to say that "you can't only Read the Word of God but you have to Speak the word of God, Trust the Word of God, Believe in the Word of God, Rely on the Word of God, Stand upon the Word of God and Lean upon the Word of God".

She talked about the Law of Confession and how you had to speak the word in order for the things that you desire to manifest itself in your life. So, Joslyn took this to heart and decided that she would no longer have negative thoughts and, or speak negatively about what God wouldn't do in her life because of all the bad that she had done in her life. Not to mention how she had contributed to being an intricate part in the demise of some other's lives.

She had decided that she would start to speak all the promises that she could remember that God says that she could have. She started with Hebrews 11:1 as it states *"faith is substance of things hoped for the evidence of things not seen"*. It goes on to say in verse 11:3 that *"through faith we understand that the worlds were framed by the word of God, so that things which are seen were not made of things which do appear.* She knew that she didn't have any one in mind, but she knew that if she spoke it, that God would provide what she needed. She also remembered reading in Ruth 1:16-17, how a personal commitment to following the Lord would always lead to redemption and life.

That promise in itself, helped Joslyn to understand that her life had indeed turned around and was headed in a different direction. She knew that she had committed her life to following the Lord and knew without a shadow of a doubt that she was going to have a good life. She read about it, prayed about it, spoke about it and most of all she walked in it. She understood that in order to really get to that place of receiving, you had to walk in it before it happened, which is faith.

Joslyn continued with her day to day routine of seeing clients, taking care of Jayla and studying God's word and walking it in. One day she and Jayla were headed to church and she told her that she was going to marry.

Joslyn still didn't have anyone in mind, but she spoke assuredly about her marriage because she had faith that God was going to provide just that. It was a desire of her heart and she knew that she was a new creature in Christ and that He would give her the desires of her heart, if it was His will.

Jayla asked, as her mom was making the statement, "who are you going to marry mommy?" Joslyn knew that Jayla didn't have anyone in mind either because she had never had the pleasure of really seeing any one in her mom's company in that capacity before. Joslyn told her that she didn't know at the moment, but God was going to provide them with a husband and father soon. Jayla sat there as Joslyn was driving with a look of bewilderment on her face. Her face was frowned and creased with lines in the middle of her forehead and then without any effort she began to smile.

Joslyn asked her why she was smiling all of a sudden and Jalya advised her that she knew who she could marry. Jayla told her that she could marry Andy James Richardson, an engineer for a large firm in Atlanta as well as a minister that came to visit their church several times during the summer for the annual events involving the youth.

Joslyn couldn't imagine why her daughter would say Minister Richardson because she didn't know that she even noticed him much. Joslyn asked her why she had said Minister Richardson. Jayla said, "Because he is very nice and we have a lot of fun when he comes and ministers to us". Joslyn was moved by her response, but she would definitely have reservations about marrying a minister. Not to mention the fact that she hadn't really had a personal conversation with him and knew nothing about his status. She told Jayla that she didn't think so and Jayla wanted to know why. She didn't have an answer for her thus causing her to change the subject.

As they traveled along, Joslyn was thinking to herself about what Jayla had said in response to Minister Richardson. She began to question why she had reservations about a minister. What made him any different from any other man and what terrified her in regards to it? She couldn't come up with any valid answers to those questions because the woman she was now had no reason to be reserved about it.

It was winter, and Christmas was approaching rapidly so the youth at church were preparing for the annual Christmas pageant. Minister Richardson was the guest speaker at church and the youth were very excited that he was coming at a time other than during the summer. All of the skits and speeches were given out and the planning for the pageant was going quite well. Joslyn had decided to volunteer to help with costumes and prop set up if needed. While she was in the dressing room looking for Jayla's scarf, she heard voices talking in the hall way.

She began to eaves drop on what was being said. She noticed by the tone of their voices that it was Pastor

Welters and Minister Richardson discussing his private affairs. Pastor Welters was asking Minister Richardson how he was getting along since the long drawn out divorce a couple years ago with his ex-wife. Minister Richardson, said, "Everything is fine, but I'm waiting on God to send me the woman that he has prepared just for me as my bride".

They talked a little more about superficial things and then they walked toward the sanctuary to check on the lighting and the sound. When they walked away, Joslyn couldn't believe that he was a divorced man and wasn't seeing anyone. She also reflected on the fact that her daughter thought very highly of him.

It was Saturday and the pageant would begin promptly at seven o'clock in the youth sanctuary. Joslyn never saw clients during the holiday season because she wanted to be sure that those times were special for Jayla. She knew that this year's pageant was probably the best of all to Jayla as she was the leading lady Mary, the mother of Jesus, in her skit "Jesus is the Messiah". So during this time Joslyn helped with the costumes and made sure that everyone was in their proper places in back ready to go on stage when their turn came.

The pageant began and everyone did a splendid job in saying their parts. The kid's performances were outstanding and Ms. Jayla was an excellent Mary in her skit. The pageant was finished and Joslyn was backstage helping pick up items that the children had left all over the floors and in the chairs. Normally everything has to be cleaned and repositioned after every event because Pastor Welters didn't like coming in the next day after an event and seeing things in disarray. However, that night he came back stage and instructed all the volunteers to leave and go home with their families.

He stated that the kids had done such remarkable performances that he didn't want them to have to wait until the volunteers, which consisted of most of the parents, to finish cleaning up to celebrate their success. As Joslyn was gathering her purse she called to Jayla to leave and she noticed that Minister Richardson was standing alone in the corner by the exit door reading a memo of some sort.

Suddenly, as she stood there watching him, the thoughts of the conversation that she had heard Pastor Welters and him having entered her mind yet again. She couldn't understand why he was single and what did Pastor Welters mean when he said his divorce was drawn out? She had heard through the grapevine that he worked a lot out of town and that he was a very kind and humble man. But, other than that she heard virtually nothing about what caused his marriage to end.

Joslyn's daydream was interrupted by Jayla yelling for her to hurry and come on so they could get ice cream at Cold Stone. So Joslyn continued to gather her things and headed towards the exit door where Minister Richardson was standing reading. As she walked past him she said, "good night" and he said the same. She was really nervous as she walked by and couldn't understand what or why she was feeling any kind of way in regards to him.

After she and Jayla sat for more than an hour talking about the highlights of the pageant while eating their ice cream, they decided that it was time to go home and get prepared for a day of shopping for the presents that they had written on their Christmas lists.

Jayla would always have a list that was about as long as the paper itself, but Joslyn would never allow her to purchase everything on that entire list. Hour after hour and store after store they shopped until finally Jayla wanted to go to the food court to get something to eat.

Jayla always loved eating from the Japanese joint in the mall regardless of how long the wait was. She really liked the way they steamed their veggies and the taste of their Teriyaki Chicken and shrimp. Joslyn ordered the same as she was too tired to even think about going and standing in another fast food line for anything.

They received their food, sat down, blessed their food and began eating while observing all the patrons in that area. Jayla would always focus on the kids that were riding the merry go round in the food court. She thought it was amusing how the little babies would jump and run around enjoying the ride. Joslyn would just eat and watch how couples interacted with each other.

While Joslyn was engaged in watching this couple that sat across from them have a disagreement about something to do with change and paying too much, she noticed that Minister Richardson was standing in the line at the Japanese joint waiting to be served. She wasn't sure if she should say anything to Jayla or not because she didn't want to interrupt his down time with a child harassing him. So Joslyn decided not to and continued to watch him. As she was watching him, Jayla happened to turn her focus towards the direction that her mom was looking.

Instantly, she realized that it was Minister Richardson standing in line and became so excited. She asked her mom if she could go over and say hi to him and invite him to come and sit with them. Joslyn was a little reserved about her inviting him to sit with them and told her that she could say hi, but did not want her to ask him about joining them. Jayla was so excited that she jumped up from her seat nearly knocking her Arnold Palmer (which is lemonade and sweet tea) on the floor.

As Jayla approach Minister Richardson, she noticed that he reached down and gave her a hug. Joslyn couldn't hear what was being said but she assumed that he had asked who she was with and where were they sitting? Joslyn noticed that Jayla was pointing towards her and Minister Richardson gave her a smile and wave simultaneously. Joslyn did the same and turned her focused back on the couple that was having a disagreement. The man had become belligerent and really rude when he spoke to the lady.

Things of this nature often frightened Joslyn because she had heard so many horror stories of innocent people getting hurt because they were in the vicinity of the incident that took place. The security guard walked over and told the man that there were families and kids in the mall and his language was inappropriate and that he would have to ask him to leave if he continued with his verbiage. Luckily, the security guard was a big man, weighing around 320 pounds with a big, shiny, bald head and broad shoulders.

The guy either was intimidated by the security officer or he decided that it wasn't really worth it to continue to make a scene. Joslyn just sat looking back and forth between Jayla and Minister Richardson and the man making the scene. Moments later, Jayla and Minister Richardson were headed towards their table. They were having a conversation that had her daughter really engaged because she was smiling and responding so well.

Although, Joslyn couldn't hear what was being said, it appeared that Jayla was very enthused by the conversation. As they approached the table, Jayla said that she had invited Minister Richardson to sit and eat with them and wanted to know if it would be okay. Joslyn thought to herself it had to be okay because he was already standing their holding his tray of food. She looked at her little girl and said, "of course he can join us", knowing that she was a little uneasy around him and had told Jayla not to do it in the first place.

They sat, ate and talked about everything from the pageant, to basketball, and school. He was very good at keeping Jayla interested in the conversation, unlike Joslyn was. She would want to have conversations with Jayla but she would get bored or she didn't want to talk to her mom about many things.

After finishing their meal, they disposed of their trash, said how they enjoyed his company and headed home for their usual hot tea and late night movie watching as they did each time after long hours of shopping. The next morning, while lying in bed, Joslyn thought about Minister Richardson. She thought about his appearance which she had never reflected on before.

He was not as tall as most men that she found herself attracted too. Wait a minute, she thought, when did she become so attracted to Minister Richardson? She never looked at him in that way because he was a minister and for some reason she thought that it made him different in some strange way. It did make him different from the men that she had chosen to spend her time with, because he was a man with morals and values and most of all had a love for God; not to mention her child absolutely adored him. But, he was still a man.

This man had the most gorgeous smile and the warmest personality that would captivate any woman that he came in contact with. Joslyn started to feel a real warm feeling inside, somewhat like butterflies flopping around in her belly. She had this feeling like that of a fourth graders that has a crush on little Timmy and would smile every time someone mentioned his name or he came around. This was very odd for Joslyn because usually if it was a man she had her sights on, she would immediately let him know in some way.

She was very straightforward when she wanted some attention, conversation, or time with the opposite sex. However, she wasn't that person anymore nor did she want to do anything that remotely resembled that person. Wow, she thought, as she lay there, I have a crush on Minister Richardson. It has been a long time since she had a crush on any one and she didn't know how to channel this new feeling that she was experiencing.

She was so excited though because this confirmed the change that she knew that had taken place in her life. Her thoughts were interrupted by Jayla bursting in her room to inform her that she wanted to go over to her Aunt Terrell's house to help them with Christmas decorations and that she wanted to sleep over. Terrell's house was Jayla's home away from home and Joslyn never had a problem with her being there because Terrell's rules were the same as hers. Joslyn told her to be ready to leave in thirty minutes and she would drop her off.

After dropping Jayla off at Aunt Terrell's house, Joslyn decided to go by the church to chat with some of the mothers that were there getting ready for Sunday's service. She saw Mother Maxie sitting in her usual area folding some napkins that were going to be used for the luncheon after service.   She walked over and started to have a conversation with her about church and the pageant. Joslyn was just making small talk with Mother Maxie because she was trying to figure out how to ask her about Minister Richardson.

Mother Maxie was talking and talking and Joslyn hadn't heard a word because she had zoned out thinking about what to say. Mother Maxie cleared her throat and said, "honey did you hear me"? Joslyn said, "I am sorry I got lost there for a moment, what did you say"? "I said, what do you think of Minister Richardson"? Joslyn was surprised that Mother would asked that question because she was going to ask her the same question. Joslyn said, "What do you mean, what do I think"?

Mother was one of those women that said what she meant and meant what she said. She stated, in a firm and direct tone, "Child don't play with me and don't think I'm so old that I don't understand men and women stuff; I'm old, not dead and I have not been old all my life! I see how Minister Richardson looks at you and I never saw anything in your eyes concerning him until today when you walked in here". This took Joslyn for a loop because how could she have known that she was coming in there to talk to her about him.

Joslyn didn't know what to say in response to what Mother was saying but she did smile at what she said. Mother went on to say that "he is just a man that loves God, he loves the people of God and he is a family man; isn't that what you wanted to ask?" Joslyn was speechless at first because she felt like she was the subject of a prank or something. Then she was finally able to speak. She told Mother that out of nowhere she had become very attracted to him and didn't know how to channel what she was feeling. She knew that he was a man but didn't know how to approach this situation.

Mother told her to do nothing. She told her that the bible says in Proverbs18:22, *"Whoever finds a wife finds a good thing, and obtains favor of the LORD!"* "This means that you don't go around chasing after no man. You don't put yourself out there and do all those nasty things that women do to get a man.

Women go around here doing all sorts of things with men and giving them all they got and then he leaves them with one of three things, a broken heart, a baby or a disease that they can't get rid of and he is off finding the next victim! Let the man find you!

It's okay to talk with him and go to dinner with him but that is far as it needs to go! Do you hear what I am saying to you?" Joslyn felt like she was being scolded by her mom when she got her hand caught in the cookie jar. She didn't expect Mother to go there; she just wanted simple advice about how to channel her having a crush him, geesh!

Joslyn was very respectful to Mother Maxie and answered, "Yes ma'am" and hurriedly change the subject.

She talked a little more about Sunday's service and told her that she needed to go because she had to take care of a few things before the day stole away from her. She hugged Mother and told her thanks for the talk and left quickly.

When Joslyn made it to her car, she was almost in tears as she thought about what Mother had said in regards to women and men. She had women pegged so right when it came to all that they would do to get a man's attention and what he would do in return.

Joslyn was the first to admit it because unlike many others, she didn't have a problem admitting her flaws and shortcomings to herself anymore. She knew that God had brought her from a long way and she was so thankful that she wasn't that person any more.

Sunday service was great and the luncheon following it was exceptional. Joslyn was unusually quiet because she had so much on her mind. She knew that after the New Year she had to resume with her clients and get back to life as usual. She had less than two weeks more off work. The New Year was approaching fast and she didn't want to start another year off with the same old baggage and stuff weighing her down.

She had indeed given her life to Jesus and she was living a life that she knew was pleasing. She wasn't altogether perfect, because no one was, but she was making strides towards perfection as the scripture says in Philippians 3:14, *"I press toward the mark for the prize of the high calling of God in Christ Jesus."* She knew that if she kept walking in His Will and Way that she would get the prize that is promised and that is to be in Heaven with God.

She also knew that if she continued in His Will and Way that He would give her the desires of her heart, even though there was a time that she didn't think this would be possible. She had to keep moving forward and most of all she really needed to stop looking back at her past to try to determine what her future would be.

It was December 31st and watch night service would begin at 9:00 pm. It always started around nine because Pastor Welters would give people time to get there before the clock struck twelve. At this particular service there were praise dancers, singers, musicians, skits and speakers from all over that came to say good bye to the old year and to celebrate the new one. The service was awesome and many people surrendered their life to the Lord.

Pastor Welters did something that he had never done before. He had a big tin barrel outside with a huge fire brewing inside and stated that the Lord had laid on his heart to do something different. He had the ushers pass out pieces of paper and told the congregation to write everything they wanted to leave behind on it and bring it up to the alter and they would pray and then burn it in the barrel. He gave everyone time to write down what they wanted to discard from their lives. Everyone began writing fervently. Joslyn sat for a moment and began writing as well.

She wrote, "I don't want anyone else's husband, boyfriend, man or anyone that is attached to any one in any way being a part of my life anymore!" After she wrote it down, she did as instructed and took it to the altar and stood there as prayer was about to commence. As she stood waiting for all the others to bring theirs to the altar, she was praying in her spirit asking for forgiveness yet again.

However, this time she truly felt a sense of true repentance and being forgiven. She had repented before as many people do, and go back and do the same thing over and over again. But, at this moment, she realized and God did too, that she really was sorry and didn't want that in her life any more. The weighted feeling that she so often felt was totally gone and she knew that things would be so much better from that moment on.

It was New Year's Day and many people were cooking out, shooting fireworks and just spending time with family. Joslyn went over to Terrell's house as Jayla was there playing with all the kids in the neighborhood. The adults sat around talking about the good ole' days and how much fun they had growing up.

Most of the discussion was about how men would treat women and how they sat and took it because they didn't want the woman across town to have him, knowing that he was with her as well. Immediately, Joslyn changed the subject. She didn't want to rehash anything that resembled who she used to be. She also did not want to look back in time and have to tell her auntie's and their friends how they played a part in her life being so messed up because she saw what they went through.

So Joslyn started talking about how she was going to get married and how her life would be. This shut everyone in the room up. You could hear several pin drops throughout the entire room. Joslyn's Aunt Lizzy, her mom's sister, wanted to know who this mysterious man was. Joslyn told her that she didn't know yet but it was sure to happen. Everyone kind of laughed and gave her that "yeah right" type of look and continued on with a discussion that Terrell had started about her going to nursing school.

Joslyn was really offended that they mocked her and didn't take what she was saying seriously. She told Terrell that she would be back later to pick up Jayla and went to Dillard's in Enterprise for their annual New Year's Day sale.

While walking through the store she noticed all the sales that they were having and found some great deals on some items for Jayla. She looked around for a couple hours and decided that she would leave. As she was walking to her car, she noticed that Minister Richardson was walking to his car on the next row. She wondered if he had noticed her and if not how could she get his attention to say hi.

But at the moment she remembered what Mother Maxie had said about not doing anything. She knew that a man was to find a woman but the bible didn't say that a woman couldn't say hello to a man first. So Joslyn walked through the path of two cars to get to the next row. She surprised Minister Richardson because when she said, "hey stranger" he looked a bit spooked. His face turned a little red as his complexion was an olive tone.

He smiled, and said, "Hi, you startled me, where did you come from?" Joslyn told him that she had come to Dillard's for their annual sale and that she noticed him walking to his car and wanted to say hello. He said, "That was nice" and began to smile uncontrollably.

Joslyn thought to herself, why is he smiling like a chesire cat and why is he just standing there dumbfounded? She knew that this would be the most opportune time to ask him what he did in this spare time.

She asked, "So Minister Richardson, what do you do for fun?" He threw her for a loop when his response was, "I am not looking for a relationship." Joslyn became really irritated by his response because she wasn't asking for a date nor was she asking to get married, she simple just asked what does he like to do for fun.

She stated that very thing to him too and he laughed it off and they talked for more than an hour in the parking lot. He received a call from his mother and had to leave because she had been waiting on him for a while to take care of something for her.

They said their good byes and departed without exchanging any numbers, email addresses or anything. Joslyn walked back to her car feeling a little defeated because he said that he wasn't looking for a relationship. The crush that she had on him was even more apparent now to her and to him because she said something to him in the parking lot. Joslyn went back to Terrell's house picked of Jayla and headed home for her last week of her short sabbatical to do absolutely nothing.

It was approaching the weekend and she noticed that Minister Richardson was due to speak at the 7:30 service on Sunday. Joslyn usually didn't go to that particular service. She would always attend the 11:00 service. However, she decided to go to the 7:30 service just to see his face.

She had to admit to herself that she did feel a little rejected and didn't like how that felt but she knew that she would be okay. During the service, there is a segment that's called meet and greet where the congregation would walk around and hug each other and tell them how glad they are to see them.

During this segment, Joslyn noticed that Minister Richardson was trying to make his way over to her area as she had made eye contact with him a few moments earlier. She didn't want him hugging her because she knew that she had a crush and that would be misleading in her mind, so she made a point to walk in the opposite direction to be sure that she wouldn't be able to hug him. After that segment, a young lady sang a solo entitled "God Still Heals". This song must have made a profound effect on Minister Richardson because when he got up to give the spoken Word for that hour, he was so outdone with tears that he could barely speak.

He tried to speak but now he was crying as if he had just heard that a loved one had gone to be with the Lord. About ten minutes passed and he had gotten himself together and was able to give the Word that God had given him. It appeared that he had gotten some type of breakthrough from the song that had been performed.

After service, Joslyn and Jayla went to Terrell's house for Sunday dinner as they did most Sundays. Everyone was sitting around eating and talking when the doorbell rang. When Terrell answered the door, she said that it was someone for Joslyn and that they wanted to speak with her. Joslyn got up from the table and proceeded to the front door and it was a lady that said she was Minister Richardson's sister. Joslyn didn't recognize her because she didn't know much about his siblings or any of his family for that matter.

Anyway, the lady stated that her name was Larissa and that he had given her his number and email address to give her. Joslyn was taking by surprise because she distinctly remembered him saying that he wasn't ready for anything that had to do with a relationship. Larissa told her to contact him because he was expecting it. Joslyn said, "Thanks", closed the door and sat on the couch contemplating whether she should or should not contact him. She decided that she would, but wouldn't do it right away.

A few days went by and she decided that she would email instead of call because emails was so not personable. She sent him an email stating that his sister Larissa had given her his contact information and she wanted to know if he in fact had given it to her to pass along. Hours went by and there was no response to the email.

Joslyn got a little impatient and decided that she would call his number instead. As she dialed his number, her stomach was doing flips and her palms were sweating like crazy. The phone rang, one, two, three, and on the fourth ring as she was getting ready to hang up, she hears a hello. She said, "Hi this is Joslyn and your sister Larissa came by my sister's house the other day and gave me your contact information to contact you. I emailed you and never got a response, so I decided to call."

Joslyn said all of this in one breath like she was a salesman trying to con someone into buying something. When she finished he said, "Breathe!" They both laughed and he confirmed that he had given her the information to pass along. Joslyn wanted to know why he couldn't do it himself and he said that he would explain that later. They talked for more than an hour on the phone and decided that they would meet that coming Saturday and do dinner and a movie. Joslyn hung up and was very excited about their date, but was fearful as well. She had so much planning to do; what would she wear, how would she do her hair, what fragrance would she put on, all became questions in her mind.

Saturday had finally come and Joslyn was so excited about going on a date with Minister Richardson. She had butterflies all week and would role play in her head how the evening would go. He arrived at her home around seven o'clock to pick her up. She was waiting in her foyer, sitting in front of the bay window next to the front door. She saw Minister Richardson as he drove up in his black, freshly waxed, and shined Infiniti Q45. She thought his car was very sexy and he looked so nice driving it.

She wanted to rush out the door to meet him but she knew that allowing him to come up and ring the doorbell was the proper way to go. She watched as he got out of his car and walked up to the front door to ring the doorbell. She waited for a moment before opening it; she didn't want to seem too anxious about spending time with him. She finally opened the door and beckoned him to come inside. He assured her that they needed to hurry as they didn't want to miss their reservations at Ruth Chris. Joslyn didn't hesitate any longer as she loved the potato pie at Ruth Chris.

They reached the restaurant, valet parked the car and proceeded to go inside and enjoy their evening. They ate their meal, while they talked about any and everything. Joslyn told him about her ambitions to one day have her own practice because now she worked for a firm, but always desired to branch out on her own. He talked about his job and how demanding it was. He really loved what he did for a living as an engineer but it kept him away from home a lot and that was the part that he didn't like.

They talked about everything except past relationships. Joslyn really wanted to know what happened with his ex-wife but knew she couldn't ask those types of questions because you have to allow a person to reveal that in their own time. She also felt that he wanted to know personal information about her but he didn't seem like that kind of person that would get personal with her on that level either. As she sat listening to him talk, she knew that he was so different than anyone that she had ever been on a date with before.

There was no pretense in who he was and he was really interested in what she had to say and not just making small talk before he went in for the kill and tried to make a move on her. A few hours had gone by and it was getting late so they decided to call it a night. Joslyn was a little nervous about how the date would end, because this was so new to her. When they arrived at her place, he came around and opened the door for her and escorted her to her front door. They said their good nights and how they enjoyed the evening and she went inside and he left.

The next day, she thought about how nice the date was and equally how nice Minister Richardson was. He was a perfect gentleman and he really lived up to whom he said he was in Christ. Joslyn often wondered that about him because so many "so called" men of the cloth were doing things men of the world would do.

They were cheaters, beaters and abusers of women, especially their emotions and she would and could never date a man that proclaimed to be man of God and turned out to be the devil himself. Although, she had dated one that said he went to church and how faithful he was in going and turned out he was not as faithful as he let on. Joslyn really wanted to see Minister Richardson again, but she could not be the one that initiated that because she would appear to be a desperate woman.

Sunday service was great and Joslyn was extremely excited. She was always excited to go to church and praise the Lord, but what she was feeling this particular Sunday had a lot to do with a certain man named Andy James Richardson. She couldn't get his smile out of her mind nor could she get the smell of the cologne "Issey Miyake" that he was wearing out of her nostrils. She knew he would call again, but wondered when.

A day or so past and she hadn't heard from Minister Richardson and now she was becoming discouraged. She started to wonder if he had heard about her past or if he was no longer interested in her. She decided that she would let

God take care of this situation and if he was meant for her it would indeed happen in God's timing.

She was back at work and seeing clients and really didn't have the time while she was in the office to focus on her own issues because she had so many clients that really needed her undivided attention. Even though many of her clients had the same issues, she had to give them the attention that their money afforded them. She hadn't seen Elaine in a while but today she would and she could get an update on how things were going in her life.

Elaine arrived at three o'clock and this time she seemed a little more upbeat. Joslyn was excited to see her this way and wondered what had happened since she saw her months ago. Joslyn asked her to have a seat and before she could say anything Elaine began to tell her about what was going on. Elaine told her of her experience with going to church. She told her that she had gone to church, a revival, shortly after her last session.

She told her that a guest speaker by the name of Prophetess Barbara Gaines from Orlando, Florida, was there and how what she said to her changed her life. She said that in all these years she thought that she needed counseling for all the issues that she had with her husband Dexter, but all she really needed was for her to allow God to be the head of her life and walk in His will and everything else will fall into place. Joslyn was moved by this because unbeknownst to Elaine, she had experience this same type of reality from Prophetess Gaines as well.

Elaine went on to explain how when Prophetess Gaines called her up and started to reveal to her about her life and how things were going, she was astonished because she didn't know her nor had she ever heard of her until her friends asked her to go to the service.

Elaine was so impressed with Prophetess Gaines that she pleaded with her husband Dexter to join her on the last night of the revival. He was a little hesitant at first, but agreed to go. She went on to tell Joslyn that Dexter went and this time Prophetess Gaines called them both up and really ministered to the both of them about marriage and how a man should be with his wife. Prophetess Gaines had shared many scriptures with them on that night that really made Dexter think in a way that he had never before.

She quoted, *""Giving thanks always for all things unto God and the Father in the name of our Lord Jesus Christ; submitting yourselves one to another in the fear of God. Husbands, love your wives, even as Christ also loved the church, and gave himself for it; that he might sanctify and cleanse it with the washing of water by the word, that he might present it to himself a glorious church, not having spot, or wrinkle, or any such thing; but that it should be holy and without blemish. So ought men to love their wives as their own bodies. He that loves his wife loves himself. For no man ever yet hated his own flesh; but nourishes and cherishes it, even as the Lord the church: for we are members of his body, of his flesh, and of his bones. For this cause shall a man leave his father and mother, and shall be joined unto his wife, and they two shall be one flesh. This is a great mystery: but I speak concerning Christ and the church. Nevertheless let every one of you in particular so love his wife even as himself"* in Ephesians 5:20-21; 25-33.

After she finished telling us what God had revealed to her, I couldn't believe when I looked over at Dexter and he was sobbing so sorrowfully. I had never seen Dexter in this state before nor had I ever seen him cry. He was so vulnerable and even though he had not been a good husband to me, I just wanted to hold him and tell him that it was okay. But what happened next really showed me who God was and that we would be okay for sure.

Dexter confessed his sins and accepted Jesus as his personal Savior. He then turned around and apologized to me in front of more than a hundred people and promised that he would be a better man because even though he was never a good and faithful husband, I still stood by him.' At that moment, Joslyn was so filled with joy that it took every ounce of energy in her to hold back the tears that had swelled up in her.

Elaine said that even though she enjoyed coming to meet with Joslyn to discuss her problems that she didn't need her anymore because now she had a wonderful counselor and his name was Jesus and that she would be using him from now on. Joslyn was certainly okay with that because even though she was being fired as Elaine's counselor, she knew that the replacement that she chose was much more equipped to handle all her needs and would not cost her a dime. Joslyn gave Elaine her blessing and she left.

When Joslyn got home, fixed dinner for Jayla, and got dressed for bed she remember how Elaine talked about their experience at church and a warmness filled her heart as she knew that they would be much better now. She knew that it wouldn't exempt them from having obstacles in their life, but that the fact that they had connected to the right source would make it bearable. Joslyn checked her messages on her machine and there was finally a message from Minister Richardson.

He apologized for his delay in calling but he had an unexpected business trip the very next morning and hadn't got back until moments prior to his calling. Joslyn listened to his message several times and was overjoyed that what she was feeling was not the case. He didn't call because he was out of town on a business trip and wanted to wait to call her when he returned. He wanted her to call him back once she got the message. Joslyn called and he picked up on the first ring. That was not expected because normally the phone would ring at least two times before anyone would pick up. He said, "Hello" and explained about his trip. They set another date for the next evening and said good night.

It was Friday night and they agreed to meet at Olive Garden. Joslyn wanted to meet because she wanted to drive herself instead of having him come so far out to pick her up. They met and he greeted her with a smack on her lips. Joslyn's heart was doing summersaults as she did not expect him to touch her lips with his. She was caught off guard by it as well because she was wondering if this is something that Minister's do and was this sinful.

Minister Richardson noticed the look of uneasiness on her face and quoted what the bible says in 1Peter 5:12 *"Greet one another with a kiss of love."* Joslyn acted as if she wasn't thinking anything about it but he told her he knew what she was thinking when he did it. They sat, ate and talked more about their lives.

This time Minister Richardson shared with her what happened in his first marriage and said that he really didn't want a divorce but his ex-wife did and he didn't have a choice but to grant her that. He was married to her for more than twenty years and really wanted to honor his commitment that he had made to God but she had no interest in doing that. He stated that he wanted them to go to counseling but she refused to do so. She just wanted the marriage over, so here he was.

Joslyn was really reluctant to tell him about her past, but she decided to do so because this was the moment that presented itself. She told him about how competitive she was and how she used this mindset as a way of conducting her life. She told him how she dated men that were involved with someone and that included someone that was not only seeing someone, living with someone, but that also including someone that was married as well. She told him about everything that she thought was relevant when trying to establish a new relationship with someone. He sat there listening intensely.

Joslyn wasn't sure about how he was processing what was being said, but she was so glad that she had become a woman that had accepted responsibility for her actions and one that was working very hard to live a life that pleased God. After she finished sharing with him, she asked if he had any questions. He wanted to know about Jayla's father and surprisingly he had heard of him.

He also wanted to know if she was dating anyone as he had already confirmed that he wasn't. Joslyn told him that she was single and that she had decided that she wasn't going to date anyone else unless it was someone that she knew with absolute certainty that he was the man that God had prepared just for her. They continued to make small talk and again called it a night and she drove home.

On the way home, Joslyn was so happy that she had shared her life with him. She would not have to worry about him hearing it from someone else now nor would she have to wonder about his status because he shared his life as well. Day after day she and Minister Richardson would either speak on the phone or he would drive down to see her.

They had become inseparable. Jayla was really happy because she always liked him anyway, but to have him spend quality time with her and her mom was such a thrill to her. She was so happy for her mom because she could see the joy in her eyes when he was around and when he wasn't that joy was still present.

One particular evening when Minister Richardson came down to visit, Jayla was over at Aunt Terrell's house. It was a week or so prior to Valentine's Day and he stated that he wanted to share something with Joslyn that he had not shared before. Joslyn was a little nervous about what that could be as she thought that they both had laid their cards on the table at Olive Gardens. He asked if they could sit down and just talk. This really made Joslyn nervous because she was unsure about what he wanted to say to her.

What he finally said to her was so profound that she started crying as he spoke. Minister Richardson told Joslyn how when he saw her that day at the mall, why he made the comment that he had made. He went on to tell her that God had already shown him that she was supposed to be his wife but he was not going to act on it himself. He told her that after his divorce, he had dated a couple of women as well trying to fill that void that was left in his life and he had made a travesty of it because they fell apart.

He finally had a serious talk with God and told him that he would not choose anyone for himself anymore. He continued and said that he told the Lord that the woman that he had prepared for him would have to say something to him first. He was done with trying to figure this life thing out and that he really had to rely on God to do that for him. He said that he had always noticed her when he visited their church and several times wanted to say something but that would contradict the conversation that he had with God.

He told her that God had also shown her to him in a dream that she was his wife but he told God that if that was true then she had to say something to him first. " So when you came up to me and spoke to me in the parking lot, I said what I said because it dawned on me that God had done what I asked but I was refusing to believe that it was Him in that moment so that is why I said that.

Later that night, he confirmed to me that it was him and here I am. I know that we haven't dated each other long and I know many will say negative things about our relationship, but I know that this is from God and I don't want to waste any more time with it."

Joslyn was a little confused at where he was going with all of this but she continued to listen and try to control the tears that had already ruined her makeup. He then kneeled down in front of her and said that the Sunday in church when the young lady sang "God Still Heals" he knew at that moment that he loved her although he had not had a single date with her. He then took her hand and asked if she would consider being his wife.

Joslyn was crying so hard that she could not get her words to make any sense. She was trying to say yes, but again, nothing made any sense. Finally, she shook her head in agreement with what he had asked.

He held her as she cried for what seemed like hours. After she was able to calm down, he said, "I don't have a ring with me at the moment to give to you." Joslyn told him that it was okay and that for all she cared he could tie a string around her finger. So that's exactly what Minister Richardson did. He found a thread like string and wrapped around Joslyn's finger and performed a ceremony right then and there.

Even though, it wasn't the formal ceremony that would take place days later, he being a minister wanted to make a covenant with God to announced their commitment to Him and each other as soon as possible because he had an upcoming business trip that would take him away for a few months.

One day before Valentine's Day, Minister Richardson and Joslyn Carter had a small ceremony in Pastor Welter's home as Jayla, Sister Welters and her good friend Yvonne looked on. It was one of the best days of Joslyn's life. She knew that the plans that God had for her would manifest in her life if she did her part. She also knew that she finally had a man in her life that not only loved God but loved her and her daughter unconditionally.

The games that she had played all her life in regards to relationships had gotten her nowhere at all. She was broken down to be blessed. God had to strip her of her distorted mentality and renewed her with a clean heart, mind, and spirit that was suitable for whom He had for her. Life was certainly a game until Joslyn allowed Jesus to become head of her life. She did so by repenting, believing and accepting him as her Savior and that saved her life. He saved her life, changed her life and enhanced her life because she allowed Him to and the game was no longer a necessity in her life.

It Was All a Game Until...

It Was All a Game Until...

It Was All a Game Until...

www.ingramcontent.com/pod-product-compliance
Lightning Source LLC
Chambersburg PA
CBHW032124090426
42743CB00007B/462